ST. THOMAS
AQUINAS &
EDUCATION

Studies in the
Western Educational Tradition

Consulting Editor

PAUL NASH • *Boston University*

ST. THOMAS AQUINAS & EDUCATION

John W. Donohue, S.J.

• FORDHAM UNIVERSITY •

RANDOM HOUSE • NEW YORK

TO THE MEMORY OF A MASTER TEACHER
Father William L. Wade
(1906–1968)
Professor of Philosophy, St. Louis University

FIRST PRINTING

© Copyright, 1968, by John W. Donohue, S.J.

All rights reserved under International and Pan-American Copyright Conventions. Published in New York by Random House, Inc. and simultaneously in Toronto, Canada, by Random House of Canada Limited.

Library of Congress Catalog Card Number: 67–30339

Manufactured in the United States of America by The Colonial Press Inc., Clinton, Mass.

Typography by Diana Hrisinko

Foreword

Anyone who has even looked into such monumental studies of thirteenth-century intellectual history as those of a Gilson or Mandonnet must regard a little book like this one as frivolous, if not foolhardy. It is bad enough that with a page or paragraph it brushes over complicated matters that have been the subject of searching and detailed discussions in many languages. But this is done by one who is neither a historian nor a philosopher nor a theologian, although he borrows from them all. The explanation, if not excuse, for this bold behavior is that the aim of this book is one with which such scholars do not usually busy themselves. For it is the aim of those whose special interest is in the history and theory of education. The first chapter here argues that St. Thomas Aquinas deserves consideration by persons with this kind of educational concern, and the remaining chapters intend to sketch out the relevance of Thomas' thought for education. But this is a narrow focus in view of the enormous range of Thomas' writings and the fact that he very rarely deals with matters specifically pedagogical. In order, therefore, to acknowledge the spacious context of the educational implications drawn from Aquinas, the present book makes generalizing excursions into various disciplines. The writer was rescued from some of the consequences of this amateur enterprise by the kindness of colleagues at Fordham University who read all or part of the manuscript, and he would particularly like to thank Jeremiah F. O'Sullivan of the Department of History; W. Norris Clarke, S.J., and Joseph V. Dolan, S.J., of the Department of Philosophy; and Matthew J. O'Connell, S.J., of the Department of Theology.

Contents

ST. THOMAS AQUINAS & EDUCATION

· I ·

The Place of
St. Thomas
in the History of
Education

During the second half of the thirteenth century Fra Tommaso d'Aquino was, on two occasions each lasting several years, among the most distinguished lecturers joined to the masters' corporation that made up the theological faculty at Paris. The University of Paris was at that time the academic center of Western Europe and served as an alembic for refining the notable intellectual issues of the moment. One of these touched upon the very nature of the university itself. A precisely detailed history of the university's first decades remains tantalizingly inaccessible, but certain broad lines of development can be picked out. One can, for instance, see the communities of masters in the arts and in the three higher faculties of law, medicine, and theology struggling to define and stabilize the notion of a university as a kind of third force enjoying as much autonomy as it could win from civil society on the one hand and from ecclesiastical society on the other. The *studium* intended, so to speak, to be the vassal neither of the *regnum* nor of the *sacerdotium*. The university's statutes had been first approved by the masterful Pope Innocent III in 1215; subsequently and more sweepingly, by Gregory IX in 1231. One effect of these papal actions was to clarify the character of the masters' gild as a moral person charged with the conduct of its own affairs. The faculties were pleased to urge this right against the Bishop of Paris or the French king or a Parisian tavern keeper when these personages inclined to dictate. At the same time, they were equally determined that the Pope, to whose jurisdiction they were related collectively through their charter and individually insofar as most of them were clerics, should not so enlarge his influence as to diminish what we would call their academic freedom.

This theme of freedom, knotted with passion and pique, was central to the periodic disputes in medieval Paris between the majority of masters who belonged to the secular clergy and the minority who were both clerics and monks. The most prominent among the latter were the friars of the new mendicant orders, the Franciscans and the Dominicans. These orders were social entities or subgroups founded by saints and given legal existence within the total community of the Church by the Roman See. Since the authority of their intramural law and leadership was derived from the Pope, they appealed to him when they became embroiled with the seculars. Shortly before St. Thomas' first term as a Parisian doctor (1256–1259), but while he was already living in Paris, a controversy had been provoked by the mendicant masters' refusal either to observe a teachers' strike that the faculties had authorized or to take a subsequent oath that would have bound them to such an observance. This quarrel stimulated the seculars' effort to bar the friars from the corporation. Only the nudging of a papal Bull constrained the faculty of theology in 1256–1257 to admit the two luminaries known to history as St. Thomas Aquinas of the Order of Preachers and St. Bonaventure of the Order of Friars Minor.[1]

The broadsides issued against the friars by the more agitated among the seculars drew retaliatory essays from Thomas both at this time and during his second period as a professor (1269–1272). "Ought a Religious (that is, a monk or friar) to teach?" he asks rhetorically in the first of these pamphlets that appeared in 1256 (*Contra Impugnantes Dei Cultum et Religionem*, c. 2).* After canvassing the negative replies, Thomas remarks that these are all disposed of easily. As a monk a man has, indeed, the traditional duties of prayer and penance that are metaphorically suggested by the phrase "weeping for the sins of oneself and others." But since the monk is also a cleric (that is, a priest, or at least enrolled in the clergy through the ritual of tonsure), he has the additional obligation of teaching.

It is reasonable to maintain that this dispute, which

---

* For greater convenience the references to St. Thomas' writings will be inserted directly into the text and designated by conventional cues. Thus the essay referred to above is a shorter work (*opusculum*) of twenty-six chapters of which the second is cited. *S. Th.*, I, q. 1, a. 1, c. will refer to the first part of the *Summa Theologiae*, question 1, article 1, the corpus or main portion of the article. References to the replies to objections following the body of the article are indicated by "ad" with the number of the reply. Other parts of the *Summa Theologiae* are abbreviated as: I-II (first section of the second part); II-II (second section of the second part); and III (third part). *C.G.* stands for the *Summa contra Gentiles* with book and chapter number indicated. *De Ver.*, q. 11, a. 1 refers to the eleventh of the *Quaestiones Disputatae de Veritate* (Academic Disputations concerning Truth), the first article. *In lib. Eth.* (or *Pol.*), b. I, lect. 1 signifies the first *lectio* or lecture of Thomas' commentary on the first book of the *Nicomachean Ethics* or the portion of the commentary on Aristotle's *Politics* that was done by him (the remainder was done by his pupil, Peter of Auvergne). In the references to other writings, sufficient detail of this sort is given at the point where the reference is inserted.

Rashdall called a "constitutional struggle," symbolized a perennial concern for intellectual freedom, although its specific terms are now anachronistic. (Though not wholly so, for even today members of religious orders may not receive full professorial appointments in the Catholic University of Louvain.) The secular masters were at least partly motivated by anxiety for the university's independence and their own freedom of association. The friars, for their part, felt they were defending the individual who had chosen a particular expression of religious belief from unjust deprivation of academic standing and freedom of action, although the wrangles over the oath may have somewhat obscured the fundamental point.

But it was a sensitive point for Thomas Aquinas. As Father Angelus Walz, O.P., one of his twentieth-century biographers observes, Thomas was quite conscious of his dignity as a Parisian master, or "doctor," of theology.[2] Since we know from contemporary testimonies that Thomas was serenely indifferent to personal aggrandizement, we may conclude that he esteemed the mastership as the very sign and vehicle of the intellectual vocation that gave shape and significance to his life. Teaching was not, for him, simply a career and much less a mere means of livelihood. He was severe in his judgment of teachers who were motivated by a vainglorious self-satisfaction in their own performance (Quodlibet V, q. 12, *de Doctoribus*, a. 24). For teaching and scholarship constituted Thomas' way, as a Dominican, of fulfilling the common Christian calling to love God by serving others. So it is hardly surprising to find him more than once expounding a thesis drawing upon Christian spirituality's familiar distinction between the contemplative life of hermitage or cloister and the active life followed by most people. Teaching, says Thomas, is a nice blend of both styles (*S. Th.*, II-II, q. 181, a. 3, c., and *De Ver.*, q. 11, a. 4). For the teacher's energies converge upon two objects: the material that he teaches and the students to whom he teaches it. Consequently, the verb *docere*, like the English *to teach*, takes a double accusative—which should resolve any forced antinomy between a pupil-centered and a curriculum-centered school. Insofar as the teacher must, by his own study, master the discipline he would teach, his life is contemplative. Yet it is even more properly called active, Thomas declared, since this study is ultimately directed toward helping one's neighbor and the active life consists chiefly in a man's relations with his neighbor (S. *Th.*, I-II, q. 69, a. 3, c.). Indeed, this blend of study and teaching is better than mere contemplation, just as to illuminate is better than simply to shine (S. *Th.*, II-II, q. 188, a. 6, c.). St. Thomas himself, despite the staggering volume of his publications, was not one of those professors who sacrifice teaching to research. His contemporary biographer, William of Tocco, claimed that Aquinas surpassed all his colleagues in the force and clarity of his lectures and in his ability to inspire students.[3] From the time he was five years old, at any rate, Thomas' life fell into two equal parts: twenty-two years of schooling and preparation and twenty-two as a teacher and writer, for he began to lecture on the Bible, as a bachelor apprentice at Paris, in 1252.

All this is well enough. But we may still ask whether Thomas Aquinas has much title to a place in the history of education beyond this fact that he, like many others quite unknown, was an effective and dedicated teacher. No doubt he is a major figure in the histories of theology and philosophy. But he was not, as Plato and Dewey were, a philosopher who gave a great deal of attention to educational theory. Nor did he create classic codifications of established practice as Isocrates and Quintilian did. He did not chart new educational ideals for the community, as Comenius did, or for the individual, as Rousseau did. He was not the architect of new pedagogies as Socrates, Froebel, and Montessori were. He did not shape schooling by organizing administration, curricula, and methods, as did the sixteenth-century Jesuits and the nineteenth-century public schoolmen. He did not even introduce radically new perspectives on human nature or human history after the manner of a Freud or a Marx.

It is quite clear that Renaissance school practice owed much to Quintilian, for the dependence was proudly avowed. The textbooks in our elementary schools and the methods courses for teachers would not have their present form and flavor if Comenius, Rousseau, Pestalozzi, and all the other leaders of what Montessori called "the social movement on behalf of the child" had never lived. The school psychologist would not talk the way she does as she advises awed parents if Freud had never written. But it is not possible to link Thomas Aquinas in this direct way with anything in educational practice now or in the past. He addressed himself to specific problems of education only rarely and to a limited extent, although, as we shall see later, what he did say was often instructive enough. As a rule, however, he is doing either theology or philosophy and in neither case would he have been in the way of influencing educational developments directly. Philosophers do not usually have much to say about the precise aims and procedures of popular education, although some of them would like to. It is generally a people's common way of life, including the cultural and ethical ideals they profess as well as those they actually honor in practice, that largely determines what is done in education. This is not to deny that a philosopher may conceptualize the consciousness of his age or criticize or purify it. He may sometimes so catch and articulate certain perceptions or feelings of his fellow citizens as to clarify and motivate their educational enterprise. Dewey once said that this was partly his own case, and it seems also to have been true of Rousseau and Marx. But Thomas' Christian wisdom was not the kind of theory that immediately meshes with school practice, although it has some broad implications for it.

Still, there are at least two reasons for Thomas' inclusion in the story of education in the Atlantic community since his death seven centuries ago. One reason follows simply from the eminence of his intellectual achievement itself. It was the best of its kind, and its kind was once the dominant intellectualization of men's experience. The second, and somewhat more oblique, reason is suggested by the historic fortunes of Thomism during the hundred years from 1848 to the close of World War II. A bit of expansion may be in order for each of these points.

Although he died before he was fifty, Thomas left behind a mass of writings enormous enough to preoccupy many subsequent scholars into their old age. The cataloguing of these works is not even yet definitive, but the list compiled by I. T. Eschmann, O.P., and printed in Etienne Gilson's *The Christian Philosophy of Thomas Aquinas* contains ninety-eight items of which nine brief ones are of doubtful authenticity.[4] Many of the authentic items, however, are multivolumed or are collections that might reasonably be divided into several books. Under the category of *Quaestiones Disputatae* (Academic Disputations), for instance, the treatise *De Veritate* (On Truth) is listed as a single entry, although its English translation runs to three stout volumes.

This life's work constitutes the most profound and successful expression of that particular form of theistic realism that is nowadays known as scholasticism. If scholasticism be taken simply for the key conclusions to which all its chief exponents would have subscribed, it may surely be said to have significantly contributed to rationalizing and characterizing the world outlook of a good many influential people for a good many years. It should be remembered that for several centuries after Luther there were Protestant as well as Catholic scholastics. When these various thinkers dug deeply into theological or philosophical questions, they manifested many indi-

vidual differences. But even so there was a common fund
of metaphysical, ethical, and political conclusions that
they shared both with one another and with ordinary
people. More than one student has pointed out the line
in political philosophy that runs from Aquinas to the
great Anglican divine Bishop Hooker and from him
through Locke to the founders of the American Republic.[5] Indeed, on the eve of the Revolution and for some
decades thereafter, the young men at Harvard, Yale,
Princeton, and the other colonial colleges were defending
proper scholastic theses in the proper scholastic manner.
One of the treats at commencement was a public defense
by the candidates for the bachelor's degree of such
theses in logic, rhetoric, metaphysics, ethics, and theology.
This continuation of the medieval tradition of the disputation began at Harvard, where the first theses in 1642
included *Voluntas est formaliter libera* (The Will Is in
the Proper Sense Free) and *Omne ens est bonum*
(Every Being Is Ontologically Good). At the College of
New Jersey, later to be known as Princeton, the gradu-
ates of 1750 were prepared to contend that *Subordinatio
Causarum ad Infinitum procedere non potest* (A Series
of Subordinated Causes Cannot Extend to Infinity). At
Brown in 1789 they were arguing that *Generis humani
propagationi, aeque ac virtutis conservationi, pernecessa-
sarium est matrimonium* (Marriage Is Most Necessary
Both for the Propagation of the Human Race and for the
Preservation of Virtue).[6]

The study from which these examples have been
drawn amply demonstrates the pervasive presence of the
scholastic mentality in early American higher education,
and this was, of course, only one of its zones of influence.
If one should wish, then, to get some feeling for the
method and substance of scholasticism at its best, he
ought to seek out its brilliant, if brief, thirteenth-century
peak in Aquinas and leave to specialists the quarrels and
complications of scholasticism's origins and eventual de-

cline into overripeness. For scholasticism has not been a monolithic system in which uniformity of doctrine and practice eliminated counterpoint and got all participants singing the same tune. In the autumn of 1966 *The New York Times* reported that a sister teaching philosophy in a Catholic college had spiritedly declared, "Scholasticism is dead, dead, dead." And for the benefit of untutored readers the *Times* added, "Scholasticism is closely tied to the philosophy of St. Thomas Aquinas. . . ." [7] But this is too neat and would have bemused Bonaventure and Thomas, who were quite aware of their sharp differences in both methodology and conclusions.

It is true that if scholastic thinkers are regarded from a height lofty enough to render their personalities indistinguishable, they may seem alike because of that broad consensus referred to a moment ago. They do all affirm that reality is both spiritual and material and that God exists as a personal and provident creator and not merely as the ground of the universe. They are persuaded that some measure of truth can be achieved and that man's knowledge is potentially limitless, since his intelligence is not determined by one or another physical quality as his senses are. They assert the dignity of the human person, flowing from his rationality and freedom, and his immortality as well. They argue for objective standards both of what is true in thought and what is good in behavior, although these are not necessarily easily known or easily followed. If you wish to stress this community of conclusions, you can stuff all the scholastics into a single category. You could also lump Dewey, Russell, Santayana, and Sartre together by claiming that they all reject a spiritual dimension in human nature, belief in a transcendent God, and various certitudes of the common man. But this would not be an instructive procedure. No doubt the scholastic consensus was much more than a set of mutual negations, but this does not warrant a crude blurring of significant distinctions.

In fact, to speak only of philosophy among Catholics calls for three distinctions that are fiercely important for those affected. One should note, to begin with, that not all Catholics who have worked in philosophy have been scholastics. By common usage that term refers to the intellectual tradition established by medieval thinkers and is not meant for such early Christian writers as Clement of Alexandria, Origen, and Augustine. Nor will it fit Newman, Blondel, Teilhard de Chardin, Geyser, and Marcel within the last hundred years. Then we find within medieval and post-Reformation scholasticism several schools that contended so hotly with one another as to make scholasticism look like a cauldron of disputes. The Augustinian tradition of Anselm, Bonaventure, and Scotus differs significantly from that of St. Thomas and his commentators, while the systems of Ockham and Suárez were something else again. Finally, within Thomism itself there has been much animated debate among various groups, each of which claims to have correctly assessed or developed the authentic mind of Thomas at critical junctures.[8] And one might add that, while almost all Thomists have been Roman Catholics, still there are a few who are not. The distinguished Anglican theologian E. L. Mascall has often drawn inspiration from Thomas. In the America of the 1940s Mortimer Adler was widely thought of as a neo-Thomist, although better-informed scholars were not altogether happy about that. They feared that Adler's version would only confirm the popular misconception of Thomism as excessively abstract and rationalistic.

But Adler's name may serve here as the cue for turning to the second of the reasons arguing for St. Thomas' place in the study of education. A capsule history of the Thomistic revival will help to situate this properly. For while there have been many varieties of scholasticism, Thomism became within the last hundred years easily the most celebrated. It had not always been so. In the histories of art and thought the moment of purest achievement is the hardest to hold. Between Thomas' death in 1274 and his canonization in 1323 his professional reputation got some rough handling. In 1277 a number of his opinions were censured both by the Bishop of Paris, Etienne Tempier, and the Dominican Archbishop of Canterbury, Robert Kilwardby. But these were passing curiosities chiefly useful for exploding the myth of medieval intellectual uniformity. By mid-fourteenth century St. Thomas' distinction was secure. Dante, who was nine years old when Thomas died, gives him a preeminent place in the circle of twelve great thinkers who in the tenth canto of the *Paradiso* are envisioned radiating light and music. Two centuries later the Council of Trent would honor the *Summa Theologiae* as *the* great theological synthesis.

But to be honored is not the same as to be heeded. From the fourteenth to the sixteenth centuries the Dominican seminaries, or *studia generalia,* produced a great series of Thomistic commentators, including the theological jurists Soto (1494–1560) and Vitoria (c. 1480–1546), who, along with the Jesuit Suárez (1548–1617), were so much admired by Harold Laski. But in the universities, Scotus and Ockham were quite as important as Aquinas. Moreover, after 1600 Thomism was cultivated almost solely in the Dominican houses, while one or other version of Cartesianism blended with contemporary science became the popular philosophy of Catholic schools on the continent. Indeed, by the middle of the eighteenth century even the Dominicans had to be admonished by their general chapters and a Master-General to guard against novelties and stick with St. Thomas.

In the second quarter of the nineteenth century a revival of Thomism began among some Italian Jesuits and diocesan priests at Naples, a city in which Aquinas himself had once studied and taught. We may take a hint from Van Riet and, for the sake of convenience,

date this from 1848, the famous "Year of Revolutions." [9]
Italy had had a revolt of its own and in the following
year the Jesuits founded *Civiltà cattolica,* a review that
would serve to ventilate the issues raised by 1848. Their
editorial offices became a kind of center for Thomism,
which had already been smuggled into some Italian
seminaries. From Italy the revival spread about the continent and reached America, as often happens with literary and philosophical trends, several generations later.
The Bishop of Perugia, Gioacchino Pecci, had gotten interested in the movement, and when he became Pope
Leo XIII in 1878, he effectively accelerated it. In his
encyclical letter, *Aeterni Patris,* issued in 1879, he urged
his fellow bishops to busy themselves with restoring "the
golden wisdom of St. Thomas." In the following year he
prodded the Belgium bishops into creating a chair of
Thomistic philosophy at Louvain, which was Europe's
only Catholic university in the usual sense of the term.
The first incumbent of this chair was the Abbé Désiré
Mercier. In 1889 he founded at Louvain the Institut
Supérieur de Philosophie, which was destined to become
an influential center of Thomistic research.

The revival took real roots in the United States after
World War I. It expressed itself in translations from
Aquinas, in the founding of philosophical journals, and
in the publication of Thomistic textbooks and specialized
studies. Although scholastic Latin is easier than Caesar
or Cicero, it is still a technical barrier that can keep
Thomas relatively inaccessible. But in the years between
1911 and 1935 the Dominican Fathers of the English
Province issued a translation of the *Summa Theologiae.*
It was not flawless and has been superseded by the fresh
and excellent version produced during the 1960s under
the direction of the Dominican editors of *Blackfriars.*
But in its day this first translation helped to advance interest in Thomism in the United States. *Time* once re-

ported that the young Mortimer Adler saved his money
to buy each volume as it appeared.

This sort of interest was, of course, only relatively im-
pressive, for the revival was practically limited to Catholics. They turned out further translations both from
Thomas himself and from European Thomistic scholars.
There was also a respectable flow of dissertations, monographs, textbook series, and collections of readings from
Aquinas. Although scholastic philosophy had been taught
in the Catholic colleges from their nineteenth-century
foundings, it had usually been either eclectic or a diluted
Suarezianism distilled from Latin manuals. Now these
were gradually supplanted by courses aiming at authentic Thomism. In short, from the thirties to the early
fifties, to be creatively Thomistic was to be where the
action was among Catholic philosophers in the United
States. A number of journals provided a forum for those
who were exploring Thomism in some depth or trying
to relate it to modern philosophies. *The Modern Schoolman* had begun, originally in mimeographed form, in
1925. The American Catholic Philosophical Association
started publication of *New Scholasticism* in 1927, and
the American Dominicans of *The Thomist* in 1929.

But it was the work of two French scholars that gave
Thomism its greatest prestige in the wider university
world. Since both Jacques Maritain (born in 1882) and
Etienne Gilson (born in 1884) were laymen, their mere
existence made Thomism seem less like a forbidding
clerical preserve. Their books should have dissolved the
further misapprehension that Thomism is only an
apologetic for Catholicism. Gilson has been the urbane
and peerless historian of medieval thought; Maritain, the
pre-eminent Thomistic commentator on contemporary
epistemological, political, and educational issues. Both
have been interested in the theory of art and have given
a series of the Mellon lectures at the National Gallery.

Both taught at the Medieval Institute affiliated with the University of Toronto and between them have filled some of the most distinguished philosophical lectureships in the English-speaking universities. Their impact, indeed, has probably been greater in the United States than in France.

So far as educators and the general public were concerned, however, the best known of the names associated, however loosely, with Thomism were those of Adler and Robert M. Hutchins, each of whom has been the subject of a *Time* cover story. In the thirties and forties, when Hutchins was the head of the University of Chicago and Adler his associate there, they wrote and spoke extensively on education and were widely, if inaccurately, presumed to represent a kind of typical Thomistic viewpoint. They would themselves have very likely disclaimed this attribution, which more properly fits Maritain's essays on education, including his Terry lectures at Yale in 1943, *Education at the Crossroads*. One suspects, nonetheless, that even for many university people Thomism meant what Hutchins and Adler were so provocatively saying.

For there was, after all, very little exchange between professional Thomists and the rest of the philosophers in the United States. This was clear enough in 1926 when John S. Zybura published the results of a study he had made to determine the attitudes toward scholasticism of distinguished professors of philosophy in selected American and English universities.[10] Of 65 men polled, 33 replied, and it was evident that they knew little of scholasticism and cared rather less. They inclined to regard scholasticism, Catholic theology, and the faith of Catholic Christianity as three concepts nearly synonymous and equally irrelevant to the business of philosophy. Twenty-five years later, when *New Scholasticism* was commemorating its silver jubilee, the picture was not substantially different. After Gilson's 1931–1932 Gifford lectures, *The Spirit of Medieval Philosophy,* the image of Thomism would doubtless have been somewhat more sophisticated. But in his review "A Quarter Century of American Philosophy," James Collins could conclude that, so far as any real dialogue went, "scholastics and non-scholastics have deported themselves for the most part like men of different breeds." [11]

At that very moment, however, the philosophical current among Catholic thinkers had already begun to run in a new direction. By the end of World War II young French Catholic philosophers were turning from Thomism because they judged it too ordered and intellectualistic for relevance to the contemporary situation of chaos.[12] And by the close of the Second Vatican Council in 1965 this spirit was pretty well shared by many of their American colleagues. These had come to think that Thomism, understood as a complete system, was no longer satisfactory as a workable philosophy. Some simply rejected it. Others wished to preserve its central themes. A spokesman for this latter position said:

> The future of Thomism lies not in being taught explicitly as a traditional doctrine drawn directly from St. Thomas or any of the schools that claim his name. It lies rather in its playing the role of inspiration or seedbed for newly constructed philosophies put forward on the responsibility of individual contemporary thinkers or schools who have assimilated the fundamental insights of St. Thomas into new contemporary frameworks of problems, methods, language.[13]

Some of the reasons for this sort of reassessment will be touched upon later. It is enough to note now that the modern revival of Thomism crested a generation ago, and the wave has since subsided. This is most strikingly shown by the Vatican II document on the education of seminarians. From the time of Leo XIII the Popes had strongly recommended the study of Thomism, particularly in seminaries. That provoked a good deal of contention between Maximalists who believed that these statements made Thomas *the* official Catholic philosopher and theologian, and Minimalists who concluded that Aquinas was simply proposed as a reliable Christian thinker. Both views made themselves felt in the Council debate over the Decree on Priestly Formation, which was promulgated October 28, 1965. In any event, it was the second opinion that prevailed. Speaking of the seminarian's philosophical studies, the decree does not mention St. Thomas but merely observes, "Basing themselves on a philosophic heritage which is perennially valid, students should also be conversant with contemporary philosophical investigations, especially those exercising special influence in their own country, and with recent scientific progress." So far as theology goes, seminarians are advised to learn how to penetrate the religious truths "with the help of speculative reason exercised under the tutelage of St. Thomas." [14] This is general enough. The Decree on Education, which deals with common schools rather than precisely with seminaries, makes only a single and honorific reference to St. Thomas. He is proposed as an illustrious example of the Christian search for a harmony of faith and reason in the unity of truth.

The course of this development is not surprising. For one thing, the concentration on Thomism in the enthusiasm generated by its recovery was probably too intense to last for long. Besides, in a civilization as strained by complexity and change as ours is, there are bound to be forces dissolving any synthesis the moment it is achieved. But the career of the Thomistic revival has some suggestions for the student of the history of education. To begin with, we may recall that in the United States from, let us say, 1940 to 1960 the philosophy of education of the up-to-date Catholic teacher was likely to be thought of by himself and his colleagues as Thomistic, much as secular humanists were presumed to follow Dewey.

What their respective admirers really shared with Thomas or Dewey was more likely a sum of prephilosophical convictions including a characteristic concept, religious or not as the case might be, of the ultimate nature of reality. But it was widely supposed that when a professed Catholic took part in a discussion of educational issues, he spoke from a Thomistic position that was itself interchangeable with the Catholic outlook. The first part of the supposition need not have been true. The speaker might have had little close knowledge of the Thomistic texts. The second part could not have been true. Thomas would have pointed that out since he had often criticized the Augustinian doctrine without insinuating that Augustine was less Catholic than himself.

For the philosopher of education, however, the concrete state of affairs just described points to two possible lines of inquiry. One may ask what a rounded theory of education derived from Thomas' philosophy was or might have been. If one marshals the Thomistic positions on reality, knowledge, life, man, values, and morals and draws out their educational implications, a complete and systematic statement will result. But inevitably the qualities of fullness and system will have been stressed rather than those of relevance and adaptability. Hence, the investigator might find it more rewarding to follow the lead of those thinkers who have been, to some extent, inspired by Thomas without taking over his total construction. In this case, one would look for certain master-ideas in Aquinas that have a continuing significance and can be synthesized with contemporary thought. The pages that follow are too few to exhaust either of these approaches, but they side with the second. They aim to point out certain features of Thomism that have relevance for education beyond the horizon of the medieval world. Not that one necessarily adopts these insights, but, at least, they are to be seen as speaking to living problems. Since these themes were fashioned by Thomas' reflection upon his faith and his experience, they will be more intelligible if something is first said about his life and that world in which he lived.

◇ NOTES ◇

1. Hastings Rashdall, *The Universities of Europe in the Middle Ages*, new ed. by F. M. Powicke and A. B. Emden (Oxford: Clarendon Press, 1936), Vol. I, pp. 377–385. The Bull, *Quasi lignum vitae*, was issued by Alexander IV in 1255, and Bonaventure and Thomas were admitted in submission to it the following year. See also Angelus Walz, O.P., *Saint Thomas Aquinas: A Biographical Study*, trans. Sebastian Bullough, O.P. (Westminster, Md.: Newman Press, 1951), pp. 62–69.

2. Walz, *op. cit.*, p. 152: "He was mindful of the duties of his estate, the dignity of his position of Master, and the obligations of his noble birth."

3. This paragraph reproduces several sentences from an earlier essay by the writer, "The Scholastic: Aquinas," in Paul Nash, Andreas M. Kazamias, and Henry J. Perkinson, eds., *The Educated Man: Studies in the History of Educational Thought* (New York: Wiley, 1965), pp. 115–116.

4. Etienne Gilson, *The Christian Philosophy of St. Thomas Aquinas,* trans. L. K. Shook, C.S.B. (New York: Random House, 1956), pp. 381–430.

5. See Ernest Barker, *The Political Thought of Plato and Aristotle* (New York: Dover, 1959), p. 509, and the whole of Alexander Passerin D'Entrèves, *The Medieval Contribution to Political Thought* (Oxford: Oxford University Press, 1939).

6. See James J. Walsh, *Education of the Founding Fathers*

of the *Republic: Scholasticism in the Colonial Colleges* (New York: Fordham University Press, 1935).

7. *The New York Times,* October 20, 1966, p. 12.

8. Helen James John, S.N.D., in *The Thomist Spectrum* (New York: Fordham University Press, 1966), gives an account of the disparate currents in twentieth-century Thomistic metaphysics, especially where the central theme of *being* is concerned.

9. Georges Van Riet, *Thomistic Epistemology: Studies Concerning the Problem of Cognition in the Contemporary Thomistic School,* trans. Gabriel Franks, O.S.B. (St. Louis: B. Herder, 1963), Vol. I, p. 33.

10. John S. Zybura, *Present Day Thinkers and the New Scholasticism: An International Symposium* (St. Louis: B. Herder, 1926).

11. James Collins, "A Quarter Century of American Philosophy," *The New Scholasticism,* XXV (January, 1951), 46.

12. This is the judgment of a distinguished Thomistic metaphysician, Joseph de Finance, S.J., in "A Report on French Philosophy," *The Modern Schoolman,* XXV (November, 1947), 26–27.

13. W. Norris Clarke, S.J., "The Future of Thomism," a paper presented at a Conference on Philosophy in an Age of Christian Renewal held at the Center for Continuing Education at Notre Dame University, September 6–10, 1966. A similar view is voiced by a Dominican who would date the decline of European interest in Thomism as early as 1940. Raymond J. Nogar, O.P., writes: "Thomism had fallen upon evil days, not because its basic insights are invalid, but because many areas of its system are no longer acceptable. . . . By 1940, Thomism as a system was dead in Europe. But if Thomism as a system was dead, Thomism as a priceless fountain of realistic insights was more alive than ever" (*The Lord of the Absurd* [New York: Herder and Herder, 1966], pp. 62–63). See also the instructive article by Joseph Donceel, S.J., "Philosophy in the Cath-

olic University," *America*, CXV (September 24, 1966),
330–331, and the letters commenting upon it, *ibid.*,
CXVI (January 21, 1967), 99–114.

14. "Decree on Priestly Formation," in Walter M. Abbott,
S.J., ed., and Joseph Gallagher, trans. ed., *Documents
of Vatican II* (New York: Guild-America-Association
Presses, 1966), n. 15, p. 450, and n. 16, p. 452. See
also Xavier Rynne, *The Fourth Session: The Debates
and Decrees of Vatican Council II September 14 to
December 8, 1965* (New York: Farrar, Straus and Gi-
roux, 1966), pp. 180, 182.

·II·
The World
St. Thomas Knew

Historians sometimes worry about the conventional practice of slicing up the story of mankind into discrete ages and epochs. For in history, as R. G. Collingwood remarked in his *An Autobiography*, there are no beginnings and endings. "History books begin and end, but the events they describe do not." This serves to remind us, should we be liable to forget, that the medieval era evolved out of the ancient and the modern out of the medieval. Nevertheless, evolutions of this sort do finally reach a point at which men can look back upon an earlier period and judge it to have been, in some reasonable sense of the phrase, a world different from their own. We may suppose, for instance, that St. Thomas Aquinas did not regard his civilization as simply prolonging that of the *antiqui*, as he occasionally called the Greeks and

Romans. And we may likewise suppose that American Catholics or Lutherans will, in many respects, feel more at home with Thomas Jefferson than with Thomas Aquinas or Martin Luther. For even though the distinctive religious perspectives that give their lives ultimate meaning are shared with Aquinas or Luther and not with Jefferson, still Jefferson is a "modern" man in a way in which the other two are not.

In short, it is fair to say that St. Thomas belonged to another world than ours, to that period of cultural developments that can be thought of as standing between Greco-Roman times and our own. He lived, indeed, at the very zenith of the complex and evolving set of eras that we call the Middle Ages. If, then, we would even partially understand his life and his work with its characteristic strengths and limitations, we must make an effort to think ourselves back into that thirteenth century. This is by no means easy even for the professional student of medieval affairs. For as Joan Evans observed in the Preface to her valuable *Life in Medieval France,* the history of the Middle Ages is like a great tapestry on which many figures appear against a shadowy background, although close study of those shadows will reveal a thousand details that help to explain the figures. The present writer is not competent to enter upon such details even if there were space for them here. The intention at this point is simply to make use of those findings of medieval scholarship that will suggest certain features of the world Thomas knew, particularly the aspects with some relevance for the theory and practice of education then and now.

THE OUTLINES OF THOMAS' LIFE

The difficulty of seeing a medieval man in clear light is certainly felt in Thomas' case. His own writings, al-

though awesomely extensive, are also singularly impersonal. This enhances the impression they make of a line
of thought proceeding with untroubled rationality. But
it also means that Thomas' works reveal nothing about
their author. We are apt to find this objectivity particularly alien, for nowadays if philosophers do more than
analyze language, they are apt to begin, as artists do, with
the human subject and to ask what their experience
means for themselves.[1] One will sift the *Summa* in vain,
however, for details of Thomas' inner or outer life. All
that is known for sure about him can be contained in a
short book, and much that is basic remains obscure. The
day and month of his birth are unknown, and even the
precise year has been debated. The exact route of his
travels and the dates of his lectureships in this or that city
cannot now be determined. But from one point of view
these gaps are not really crucial. The legacy of his writing demonstrates the central fact: that he lived for study
and teaching as a Vermeer, whose chronology is also in-
distinct, may be said to have lived for painting.

Thomas was born, most likely in 1225, in the castle
of Roccasecca, placed midway between Rome to the
north and Naples to the south.[2] These two cities were
linked by a 143-mile stretch of the Via Latina, which,
not far from Roccasecca, passed by both Montecassino
and the small ancient town of Aquino, from which
Thomas' patronymic is derived. This whole countryside
was in the lower half of the Italian peninsula, which,
with the island of Sicily, formed the Kingdom of the Two
Sicilies.

On the map of Europe one may triangulate the area
in which Thomas' life unfolded by taking Naples, Paris,
and Cologne as the points. When he was about five years
old, his parents enrolled him in the celebrated Benedictine abbey of Montecassino—whether as an oblate or
simply as an intern student is not now known. Some of
Thomas' contemporaries judged that the family hoped

this youngest son might one day become the abbot and thereby put his relatives in the way of sharing the monastery's revenues. If so, they were to be disappointed. It is most likely that Thomas' preliminary education in letters and piety at the abbey took place between 1231 and 1239. In the autumn of 1239, however, he went for his arts course to the University of Naples, founded a year before his birth by the controversial Emperor Frederick II, who was half Sicilian and half Hohenstaufen. The university had been established partly to serve as an antipapal voice opposing the amplification of the Pope's powers by the Bologna canonists. In fact, Rashdall dismissed the Naples institution as a "mere department of the state," which deserved no place in the history of medieval thought.

Thomas' mother was a Neapolitan of Norman descent, so the city in which he studied from about fourteen to eighteen was not entirely new to him. But the intellectual universe opened up by his studies was a fresh one. Frederick, who had an inquiring mind, had oriented his university toward the study of Aristotelian science and philosophy, which represented at that moment a new and advanced current. The cultural unity of thirteenth-century Europe is suggested by the fact that the teacher who introduced Thomas to Aristotelianism was a certain Peter of Ireland. Because Latin was a common academic tongue, scholars could lecture anywhere, and a decade after these Neapolitan years Thomas himself would be teaching in Paris although he spoke no French.

In Naples, besides the meeting with Aristotle so important for his thought, Thomas had an encounter with the Dominicans, which was important for his life. In 1243 he entered the Order of Preachers that St. Dominic had founded a generation earlier. The friars sent him first to Rome and thence to Bologna, but he never reached that city. For his mother and brothers, mightily displeased by this unseemly choice of a mendicant vocation, had him intercepted and shut up now in one, now in another of the hilltop castles of his native region. The moral sense of these turbulent people was murky indeed, and they are said to have sent a girl to seduce Thomas in his cell. But, the story continues, the attempted diversion failed when he forcibly put her out and resumed his study of the Bible and Aristotle. This indestructible patience finally overcame his tempestuous family, and he was released in 1245.

The friars thought it best not to detain him in Naples, and so Thomas was dispatched to Cologne in the lower Rhineland for his studies. The details of the journey are unknown. He may have gone first to Paris, a trip of some 800 miles, largely on foot, and then to Cologne, another 250 miles or so to the northeast. Cologne was then the leading city of Germany, and at their monastery of the Holy Cross the Dominicans had a celebrated *studium generale,* or house of study, chiefly for the education of their own members. Its presiding genius was a Swabian, Brother Albert, a polymath whose contemporaries called him the "Great" because of his distinction in natural science, philosophy, and theology. He was older than Thomas, whom he outlived by six years, and, in their day, Albert was the more renowned. He too eagerly exploited the newly recovered Aristotelian writings, and Thomas continued this interest along with his work in theology during the Cologne years, which lasted from 1246 (or 1248) to 1252. Thomas' ordination to the priesthood probably occurred during this period, and his first publication may also date from that time. It was a richly dense essay in metaphysics called *De Ente et Essentia* (On Being and Essence).

In 1252 Thomas went from Cologne to the hub of the academic world, Paris, which was *the* university. He lived at the Dominicans' *studium generale,* which was part of their famous convent in the Rue Saint-Jacques.

At first his status was somewhat like that of a graduate teaching assistant. He was called a bachelor since he already possessed his *baccalaureatus* and was aiming for the *gradus* of a master in theology. Only a few universities could grant this prestigious degree, which made its possessor a doctor, or teacher, of theology *par excellence*.

One worked up to that distinction by clearing a series of hurdles that, for the friars, included the unofficial one of the secular masters' opposition. As a bachelor of theology, Thomas was presumed to have already done some three years of arts and five of theology. He was consequently equipped for limited teaching duties, and his assignment to these by the head of his order, the Dominican Master-General, seems to have sufficed for regularization of the appointment. He worked as a sort of junior instructor associated with the Dominican master of theology, who directed the classes that were open to students from outside the Order. In his first year in this position Thomas probably lectured on selected books of the Bible, the supreme theological resource. Then for two years he lectured on dogmatic theology by following the standardized procedure of commenting on and developing themes from the four books of the *Sentences*. This was the famous and copious Augustinian theological textbook written by Peter Lombard, who had taught at Paris a century before Thomas. The four volumes of Aquinas' *Commentary on the Sentences* date from these middle 1250s and constitute the first of his three extensive theological syntheses. Fulfillment of these various bachelor's duties qualified Thomas for the licentiate or official certification for public teaching. This was in 1256, while the dispute over admission of friar doctors was still boiling and the mendicants were being denounced by their critics in pulpit and pamphlet. Sometime later that year Thomas gave the formal lecture that solemnized his emergence as a fully approved professor. In June Pope Alexander IV had remarked in a letter to the university his displeasure at the commotion raised by the seculars over this inaugural lecture. A few months later, in October, 1256, he issued a Bull (that is, a letter of greater formality and weight) constraining the faculty of theology to admit to its corporation the Dominican, Thomas, and the Franciscan, Bonaventure. There followed for Thomas a three-year period in which he wrote and taught as a fully empowered teacher of theology— master, professor, or doctor, as one may choose to call it.

At this time the Dominicans had title to only a few professorships in theology at Paris, and it was hard enough to assert the right even to these. They built up a corps of distinguished teachers, however, by sending a succession of gifted friars to take the master's degree and lecture at Paris for a time and thereafter move on to strengthen a *studium* in some other city while a rising colleague assumed the Parisian post. It may have been for some such reason that Thomas in 1259, when he was thirty-four years old, was recalled to Italy, where he lived for the next decade. A good bit of this time was spent moving from one place to another. Two Popes, Urban IV and his successor, Clement IV, often required Thomas' attendance at their *curia*. This did not mean residing in Rome but rather at Orvieto and Viterbo. For those Popes were tensely involved in political affairs, as they tried to subdue the Hohenstaufen threat embodied by Manfred, Frederick II's natural son. The Popes intended to keep Manfred off the Sicilian throne by making Charles of Anjou, the brother of St. Louis IX of France, the ruler of that southern kingdom. But in this overall climate of turmoil and risk the Popes themselves scarcely ever were able to reside for long in their own Roman See. That city was disturbed and inhospitable, and, in any case, their various businesses and campaigns kept them on the move. St. Thomas dwelt in the midst of this unrest. Now he was at the papal court, now teaching in a Dominican *studium generale*, now attending a chapter meeting or preaching in Rome, and at all times carrying on his work of study, writing, and reflection. Yet none of that contemporary chaos is reflected in his pages. His thought floated steadfastly above all the wrangles and bloodletting, for it was concerned with issues and ideals transcending any single temporal context.

Many of his major publications are dated from this decade, including some of his biblical commentaries and a theological synthesis with the rather puzzling title of *Summa contra Gentiles* (Summa Against the Gentiles), which may not have been Thomas' own title.[3] It is an extended defense of Christian teaching against opposed positions variously enunciated by ancient philosophers, Jewish and Moslem thinkers, and Christian heretics. All of these together constitute the Gentiles. During these years Thomas began work on the third and most celebrated of his syntheses, the *Summa Theologiae,* and also wrote a number of his expositions of Aristotle. He was not himself expert in Greek, but his Dominican confrere William of Moerbeke (c. 1213–1286) was, and he made fresh translations of Aristotle, which Thomas used. Another colleague who was closely associated with Aquinas from this Italian period until his death was a certain Reginald of Priverno (or Piperno), who served as companion and assistant in all his travels and work.

Thomas and Reginald journeyed to Paris when the former was recalled for a second period of teaching at the university. This was to last from January, 1269, until after Easter, 1272. The Dominicans were prompted to dispatch Thomas to Paris on this occasion because of two disputes then disturbing academic circles. One was a dreary continuation of the animosity between the secular masters and the friars. Tractates were being fired off on either side. Thomas, who had written a defense of the friars' right to teach thirteen years earlier, now produced two more short works on the same topic. In its day this controversy may have seemed to those embroiled in it to be quite as important as the second issue under debate. But for the modern reader, this latter question is much the more interesting. It was the question raised by Aristotelianism and particularly by conflicting interpretations of it. We shall look at this in some detail below.

Neither of these controversies had been fully resolved by 1272 when Thomas left Paris again. But some progress had been made, and those who opposed Aquinas' reading of Aristotle had modified their positions in light of his expositions. He had himself been fully occupied with the usual round of lectures and writing. The *Summa Theologiae* was carried forward to the completion of its long, duplex second part and further commentaries on biblical books and on Aristotle were composed. In the spring of 1272 the academic routine at Paris was halted when most of the secular masters went out on one of their periodic strikes. This pretty well limited Thomas' schedule of lectures, so he was recalled to Naples by his own province of the Order of Preachers. Here he was soon busy again with classes in the *studium* at the friars' Neapolitan convent. By December of the following year, however, he was beginning to be quite unwell and left off all writing. The third and last part of the *Summa Theologiae* went unfinished, although later someone—perhaps Reginald—rounded it out with a supplement drawn from Aquinas' earlier commentary on the *Sentences*.

Clement IV had died in 1271 and been followed as Pope by Gregory X, who, though of Italian birth, had once been a canon in Lyons. In the development of his program Gregory decided to hold a General Council in that city, and it was called for the late spring of 1274. Its agenda represented a distinctively medieval mingling of temporal and religious concerns, for the Second Council of Lyons was to consider ways of reconquering Palestine from the Moslems and of reuniting the dissident Eastern churches with Rome. Because the Pope wanted him present for this meeting, Thomas set out from Naples early in 1274 although his health was bad. By the latter part of February he had reached the castle of Maenza some two-thirds of the way from Naples to Rome. This was the residence of one of his nieces, the wife of the local count, and while stopping there Thomas felt himself growing worse. He left the castle and went to stay at the Cistercian monastery of Fossanova, which was nearby. Here, a few days later, he died on March 7, not yet fifty years old, and was subsequently buried in the abbey church.

SOCIAL AND POLITICAL FORMS:
THE ONE AND THE MANY

This summary of Aquinas' life has necessarily touched upon, or at least implied, certain aspects of the social and intellectual climate of his age. It will be useful to stop a bit longer over some of these features since in one way or another they help to locate his work.

Philosophers sometimes write in a fashion so difficult as to discourage all save their fellow philosophers. This is true of Aristotle writing the *Metaphysics* and of Thomas in certain technical monographs on such specialized topics as the metaphysics of knowledge. But in other cases, in the *Summa Theologiae,* for instance, he expressly addressed himself to students just beginning theology. Here his expositions unfold with a rather deceptive clarity and precision, and the main lines of his thought can seem remarkably accessible. This impression is somewhat misleading because even in the *Summa* the depth and import of Thomas' thought is sounded only when one has explored its historical context and the precise meanings of the Thomistic language and done some hard thinking about the arguments proposed. Still, the attentive reader need not be a professional philosopher to form some general notions of what Thomas intends.

If this reader is interested in education, he will naturally concentrate on what Thomas has to say about the human condition. In doing so he may be struck by the all-embracing or universal character of this philosophy of man. Twentieth-century philosophers are sensitive both to the relative or perspectival nature of all knowledge and to the facts of cultural diversity that anthropology has established. So they are hesitant in speaking of human nature or in generalizing openly about man. This diffidence is, however, a modern attitude and characteristic only of recent philosophy. Thomas, for his part, begins the long section that runs from question 75 to 102 in the first part of the *Summa* and is sometimes called the "Treatise on Man" by announcing succinctly that he will treat first of the nature of man and then of his origin. Elsewhere he will speak with equal directness of the ultimate goal of all men or will remark that man has two basic and natural tendencies: To know God and to live in society (*S. Th.*, I-II, q. 1, a. 8, c. and q. 94, a. 2, c.). These instances are not isolated but characteristic. Moreover, such texts are often intended as statements of a philosophical conclusion even though they may occur in the context of a theological tract.

No doubt Thomas and his contemporaries considered judgments of this sort to be the product of a metaphysical rather than a sociological analysis. Yet it is reasonable to suppose that they arrived more easily at such universal affirmations because the world upon which they reflected manifested both a lively variety of political forms and a certain cultural unity overcoming this multiplicity to some extent. It would have seemed appropriate even to a casual observer to speak of the common nature verified in the diverse members of the human multitude when experience pointed to the One of common culture underlying and unifying the political Many.

In Thomas' day the world of social structures was strongly marked both by diversity and by a dynamic of development. Twentieth-century Americans, of course, are acquainted with both these factors raised to an even higher degree. Within the national community we have the pattern of giant cities (New York's population is six or seven times that of the whole Kingdom of Sicily when Thomas lived there), affluent suburbs, and rural country-sides with a superimposed grid of equally pluralistic governmental forms: town or city administration, county and state governments, and the federal system with its three branches and complex hierarchies of agencies and bureaus. And we know that we are involved beyond our frontiers in a network of relationships to many other nations that manifest an equally dizzying diversity of social and political phenomena.

The heterogeneity in the second and third quarters of the thirteenth century was quite as real, although on a smaller and simpler scale. Moreover, these social forms were in a state of considerable flux as some evolved to greater strength and others declined. In the Italian peninsula a rich profusion of principalities shared the territory that is now a single nation. In the north were the independent cities like Florence and Milan or the maritime republics of Venice, Genoa, and Pisa. When Thomas started the commentary on Aristotle's *Politics* (which he was never to finish), he doubtless found its picture of the ancient *polis* not unfamiliar. For those Italian cities, with their populations between 50,000 and 100,000, dominating a surrounding countryside, and not only economically self-sufficient but nearly politically autonomous, were quite like the Greek city-states that Aristotle thought ideal.

In the center of the peninsula were the Papal States, in which the Pope was both civil and ecclesiastical authority. These states, which seem to us an ambiguous charge for a spiritual leader, existed chiefly to secure that leader's freedom of action in an age when kings and emperors felt entitled to help run the church. The Papal States, Pirenne remarked in his *A History of Europe*, "presented from the beginning and retained until the end the artificial character of a purely political creation, intended to assure Rome of the independence of the Holy See." [4] In the south, where Thomas was born and grew up, the Kingdom of the Two Sicilies was politically something else again. During the first half of Aquinas' lifetime this domain was ruled by the brilliant and enigmatic Frederick II. He had given this kingdom, with its cultured towns on island and mainland and its then richly productive countryside, a tight organization and an autocratic rule. He may indeed have been a freethinker who said, as Pope Gregory IX believed him to have said, that Jesus, Moses, and Mohammed were three great deceivers. But in his realm heretics were rigorously suppressed. Frederick's principal modern German biographer is partial to the "golden Hohenstaufen boy" that Frederick once was, and he defends this suppression with the customary argument that in Frederick's eyes heretics were enemies more of the state than of religion. But he does add that the Emperor was probably the most intolerant the West ever had.[5]

For Frederick was, of course, both King of Sicily and Holy Roman Emperor, and this points to further instances of thirteenth-century political diversity. For there were kings then—in France, in the Scandinavian countries, in Bohemia and Hungary, and in the Iberian lands of Castile, Aragon, and Portugal. During most of Thomas' life the French king was the saintly Louis IX whose reign from 1226 to 1270 was that of a typical feudal monarch coexisting with nearly autonomous dukes and counts. It would be a good while before the appearance of the Renaissance kings who spurred the rise of nationalism by actually conquering their own realms. Finally there was the emperor of that Holy Roman Empire that Bryce once described as something more than a notion and something less than a nation. This emperor was nominated from that federation of imperial cities and small principalities ruled by lay nobility or prince-bishops that made up medieval Germany. Because he was annointed upon taking office, the emperor had a sacral character shared by his empire that was the political expression of the unity of Christendom. Frederick, as the grandson of the great Barbarossa, was easily eligible for selection as emperor, but when he was a papal ward he had promised Innocent III never to unite in himself the roles of emperor and king of Sicily.

In 1211, however, he was chosen emperor and he transferred the Sicilian crown to his infant son so as to observe the letter of his promise. But since Frederick acted as his son's regent, he did, in fact, function both as emperor and king. That led to another round in the struggle between the empire and the papacy. This was itself a phase of the contest to determine whether the Pope should be politically subordinate to the emperor or not. The emperors had enjoyed that sort of domination in the ninth and tenth centuries, but with Gregory VII the papacy started to regain its freedom of action. Nevertheless, authority in the Church and authority in the state were not yet successfully harmonized, partly because their respective spheres of action were not clearly determined. The Pope felt entitled to instruct kings in civil affairs, and even devout kings like Louis IX enjoyed nominating bishops as much as Churchill did. Even in the thirteenth century, as Pirenne noted, the emperors still sought "to compel the Popes to recognize them as governing the universal Church." [6]

The political and military complications produced by this situation are nicely illustrated in terms of Thomas' own family. At one time his father, Landulf, was embroiled with the forces of Emperor Henry VI, father of Frederick II, who was busy securing his wife's, Constance's, hereditary right to the Sicilian crown. Later on, after Frederick succeeded to that throne and appointed Landulf to a regional office, the Aquino family was on the king's side. So when Thomas was a small boy, his father was fighting papal troops in scuffles that developed as the Pope tried to resist the aggrandizement of that single adversary who threatened on the north as emperor and on the south as ruler of Sicily. Still later, some of the Aquinati were at war with Frederick, who executed Thomas' brother, Ronald, without, according to Thomas, any appearance of justice.

These battles between the Popes and their supposedly devoted son, the emperor, remind us by their very oddity of a phenomenon beneath and beyond this foreground of political diversity. That is the fact of a cultural unity, chiefly nourished by a common religion, which made for a kind of higher internationalism to some extent unifying the Western world, which was so divided politically. There was a community we call Christendom in which Popes, emperors, and peasants were all fellow citizens. As a priest and teacher Thomas would have been quite conscious of this "one world" since it manifested itself particularly in ecclesiastical and educational affairs. Indeed, in the Middle Ages an Italian like Anselm could be Archbishop of Canterbury while an Englishman like John of Salisbury could end his life as Bishop of Chartres.

In the university world the same international spirit made itself felt. Thomas was taught by an Irishman in Naples, and he, in turn, taught at Paris. In that city, boys of fourteen or fifteen came together from all Europe to begin their arts course. The four "nations" that divided up the arts faculty and consequently these students as well were the French, English, Picards, and Normans. But the first of these included southern Europeans and the second included Germans. Intellectuals could move about Europe at will and work anywhere if they were teachers, like Thomas, or bureaucrats, like the English financial officer, Thomas Brown, and the Scottish savant, Michael, both of whom flourished at the Sicilian court—

the latter during Aquinas' lifetime. For this was an age when nationalist outlines were not yet sharply drawn, and the civilization formed under the influence of the commonly professed Christian faith was substantial enough to create an international community. The existence of that community would not amount of itself to a philosophical demonstration that the human family possesses a unity grounded in a common human nature. In any case, it was not an all-embracing community, for medieval men knew very well that there were Moslem and Asiatic nations beyond their borders. But a philosopher or theologian living in that European society might easily have regarded those basic unities as not requiring much extended proof. The common human nature could be taken more or less for granted while one got on to the knottier work of analyzing it.

THE INTERPLAY OF THE RELIGIOUS
AND THE SECULAR

If religious unity created a cultural unity and thereby integrated Thomas' world, still it did not do so perfectly, for Christians have never fully realized Christianity either in themselves or in the social institutions that are extensions of themselves. In the thirteenth century European children could come together for the incredible crusade of 1212, and no passports or surveillance at frontiers checked their pathetic march. But when their enterprise petered out in Italy, the children were cruelly exploited, and many ended up sold into Moslem slavery or compelled to prostitution.[7] Even the religious unity itself was not seamless nor unshaken. There was plenty of dissatisfaction in the Middle Ages with the way in which Christians, clerical and lay alike, so often compromised the Gospel, and this produced movements for purification and reform. Some of these were within the Christian community itself—Thomas' own Order of Preachers is one example. Others were genuinely anti-Christian, like the unhealthy resurgence of Manicheanism among the people of the Midi. In the generation before Thomas, southern France, where this doctrine had gained ascendancy, was the stage for the chilling Albigensian crusade of orthodoxy against heresy, and, if the Cathars' creed was sadly inhuman, so were the pains they suffered for it.

But granted the incompleteness and the ambiguities, it remains true that the thirteenth century knew a degree of religious unity that contributed to the creation of a shared and distinctive culture. What most strikes men of today about that civilization is the intermingling in it of the religious and the secular. Religion, the sphere of men's relationship to God, was remarkably intermingled with the secular, the sphere of men's relationship to their natural and social environments. This seems strange to twentieth-century Americans and perhaps even stranger to Europeans. For if established churches are still found in Europe, the culture of the United States, where political leaders often speak of God, manifests a greater public consciousness of religion. A synthesis of the religious and the secular would, however, have seemed wholly normal to seventeenth-century New Englanders. For in the Bay colony only church members could vote; heretical Quakers were unmercifully flogged out of town; selling goods above the decreed price could bring excommunication and consequent economic ruin, and what there was of literature and education was much colored by religious concerns.

It does not necessarily follow that when people live in a civilization where religion pervades secular activities they are better than those who live in an age when the secular is autonomous. Are the Christians of today, someone might ask, more or less authentic than those of Aquinas' day? The historian knows that he hasn't enough evidence to decide, and the believer thinks there will never be enough, for he considers that judgments of this sort do not pertain to human competence. We know, of course, that social ideals are imperfectly actualized and that much of Parisian or Roman life in Thomas' day did not reflect the Gospels, just as Harlem does not reflect the Declaration of Independence. We are, besides, repelled by a certain harshness in medieval life—the wars, the slave trade with Islam, the judicial use of torture. But then a century that has produced Auschwitz and Hiroshima is in no position to make invidious comparisons.

Putting judgments aside, therefore, we may simply note the pronounced interplay between the religious and the secular at many levels of thirteenth-century life. In the one Christendom there were the two jurisdictions— that of the Pope, the spiritual authority, and that of the king, who wielded the temporal power. But the medieval Pope was also a considerable temporal ruler who himself, on occasion, directed the engagement of his troops. Moreover, some canonists so exalted papal rights as to claim that the emperor exercised authority because the Pope had conferred it upon him.[8] In any case, the Church could judge the morality of the king's behavior since he was obliged not only by the Christian precepts binding all believers but in a special way by his coronation oath. If he transgressed the limits of his office, his subjects might be declared exempt from obedience to his rule, so that he was, in effect, deposed. This situation helped establish the principle of constitutional government under law. On their side, however, the kings and emperors could exert considerable pressure in Church affairs. For, if we may put the case too simply, the Pope may have had more canon lawyers, but the emperor had more troops. Even if a prince were excommunicated for tyranny, this hardly meant that he was deposed in fact so long as he kept a military advantage. Nonetheless, the fusion of the two zones of civil and ecclesiastical action must strike us as distinctive. Indeed, on occasion the secular was so

sacralized as to produce that most contradictory of notions, the "Holy War." Thus the Crusades. Moreover,
the temporal magistrates, as we noted in the case of Frederick II, were firm to the point of cruelty in suppressing
religious dissent because they considered it a threat to
public order. No doubt some manifestations of it can be,
which is why the Supreme Court proscribed Mormon
polygamy. But the activity of thirteenth-century Church
officials in certifying persons as heretical and handing
them over to the civil arm for punishment seems to us not
only appalling in itself but also an expression of a confused understanding of the relationship between the religious and the secular spheres.

So far as we can judge, peering through the mists
created by distance and meager documentation, the every-
day life in Thomas' times was similarly marked by interaction of the religious with the secular. Every city had
its saintly patrons and religious holidays, and so did the
individual gilds within it. The cathedral was the town's
central structure, and its very building was a corporate
action blending work and faith. Volunteer bands helped
raise the great cathedral of Chartres by hauling construction materials. "They admit no one into their company,"
wrote Archbishop Hugh of Rouen in 1145, "unless he
has been to confession, has renounced enmities and re-
venges, and has reconciled himself with his enemies.
That done, they elect a chief, under whose direction they
conduct their waggons in silence and humility." [9]

Life in these cities when Thomas lived in them was
yeasty indeed. The municipalities were expanding because their industries and their trade, both inland and by
sea, were expanding. Yet even here the tone was not entirely secular. Nicolo Polo and his son Marco were contemporaries of Thomas. But it is significant that their
journeys to the Far East on behalf of trade followed earlier ones by Franciscan missionaries on behalf of the
Cross. The influence of religion on the life even of the

mercantile city penetrated to a most unlikely area, commerce itself. For two centuries after Thomas' death the Church continued to prohibit usury, by which was meant any interest sought as profit on a loan.[10] Great banks like those in Florence were able to devise loopholes, but their practice was at least somewhat inhibited. Nowadays we expect the secular authority to curb profiteering, not the Church. It is Andrew Jackson who will defend the little man from the monster bank, not some bishop.

These fragments are cited to suggest that the central generalization about medieval society is not unreasonable. Doubtless the two dimensions of the religious and the secular were recognized, but they were seen as dimensions of the one Christendom, which was itself made possible because the membership of the Church and the membership of civil society were presumably coextensive. (In fact, the heresies showed that they were not perfectly coextensive.) That is why an Ernst Troeltsch can speak, as many others also do, of "the Christian unity of civilization . . . an all-embracing sociological system" in the High Middle Ages.[11] Some responsible students have, in fact, gone so far as to describe the medieval civil authority as a department of the Church—a situation which the post-Reformation establishments would invert by regarding the Church as a department of the state.[12]

This interplay of the religious and the secular was owed both to historical conditions and to a theological outlook. In the medieval world many political and social agencies had not matured to the degree of complexity they now possess, and so it fell to the Church to assert the rights of the citizenry against princes or to look after education and the relief of the sick and the poor. At the same time, the Christian view of the universe saw all creation, including the Church itself, as ultimately ordered to bringing men to the vision of God beyond temporal death. This did not mean that intellectual endeavor, art, science, and technology were regarded as sheerly instrumental. Surely it would be both arrogant and naive to suppose that medieval men, even if they were saintly theologians, lacked an appreciation of the intrinsic value of the human action that produced farms and cities, *Summas* and the *Divine Comedy,* the stained glass of Chartres and Giotto's Assisian frescoes. But it may be fairly presumed that these thinkers and artists were able to effect a synthesis of their creativity with the religious element in their lives because they considered the temporal to be ultimately subordinated to the eternal as an instrument to an end. It is the sort of attitude one would have found in Jonathan Edwards in eighteenth-century western Massachusetts. For even as he was stirred by a Berkshire sunset, he would see it as shadowing "the excellency of the Son of God." [13]

Not so long ago most Christians felt that this sacramental outlook (as it was sometimes called), this holding of the secular within a religious perspective, was ideal. Consequently a dim view was taken of the desacralization that in the last four centuries has seen the secular areas of politics, education, business, art and architecture, science, and literature and philosophy becoming progressively autonomous with little relationship either to the churches or to religious belief. The medieval gilds were once admired precisely because they united so many temporal and religious functions within themselves. Nowadays their responsibilities are split up among Chambers of Commerce, the NAM, unions, technical schools and institutes, social clubs, and churches. This is perhaps better, and it certainly has allowed for the fuller development of many activities that in the gild were often only embryonic or badly organized.

In any case, both Protestant and Catholic theologians have recently been applauding this coming of age of the secular, as it is often called, and the historic developments that have ushered it in. There are, of course, degrees to this approval. Some would wish to say that man's secu-

lar action is entirely independent of religious considerations because it is governed by its own purposes, which
look to no transtemporal end. Others find so radical a
secularization unacceptable but strongly defend a relative
autonomy of the secular. Indeed, since theologians have
their own arsenal of deprecatory terms, it has become
fashionable to label as Monophysitic that medieval
"merging of the world with the Church." [14] By this is
meant that just as the fifth-century Monophysites deval-
uated the humanity of Christ in their anxiety to acknowledge His divinity properly, so the medieval synthesis is
to be deprecated for having exalted the religious and the
sacred at the expense of the secular and the profane. "Today," writes the distinguished Dominican theologian,
Père Chenu, "in a universe which is consciously building
itself, we leave behind us a 'Christendom,' that is, a
Church endowed with specifically earthly powers merged
with her real powers received from Christ and used tem-
porally to spread the Gospel." [15] And he regards this desacralization of secular institutions and ways of life as a
good thing for it better preserves the character both of the
temporal and of the Gospel. The Second Vatican Council
itself took note of this newer way of looking at history in
its Constitution on the Church in the Modern World.
The autonomy of the secular sphere, it is remarked there,
does not mean that temporal affairs are independent of
God or conducted without reference to Him. But

> If by the autonomy of earthly affairs we mean that cre-
> ated things and societies themselves enjoy their own laws
> and values which must be gradually deciphered, put to
> use, and regulated by men, then it is entirely right to
> demand that autonomy. Such is not merely required by
> modern man, but harmonizes also with the will of the
> Creator.[16]

We call attention to this contemporary formulation
of the relationship between the religious and the secular

so that we may underline that quite different view that was characteristic of Thomas' world and of his own work. For while Thomas often "does" philosophy, he does it in a theological context. Apart from the commentaries on Aristotle and certain specialized monographs, Aquinas always writes as a theologian whose business it is to understand as well as possible and thereafter to expound accurately what the Christian faith has to say about God, about the origins of the universe, about the nature, dignity, and relation of God to man, and about the person and redemptive mission of Christ, who completes the divine plan of creation. So he begins the *Summa*'s survey of all reality not, as a philosopher would, with the individual man's experience of himself and his world but, as the theologian would, with God. Yet to do this work of theological meditation, to fashion this system, the theologian needs the resources of a philosophy. If he is to talk about the effects of the redemption upon human nature, he must first have come to some understanding of what he means by human nature. Thomas did, in fact, employ for his theologizing a realist and personalist philosophy that may be described, at a very high level of generalization, as continuous with the classical tradition of Plato and Aristotle.

Since Aquinas was, however, a theologian who philosophized, it has been reasonably objected that he was not a philosopher as we understand the term today. For modern philosophers are not, and could hardly imagine being, theologians doing philosophy. Nevertheless, there are two distinct kinds of argumentation in Thomas' books. Sometimes his method and assertions are strictly theological, that is to say, based ultimately on the authority of God whom the Christian believes to have spoken and acted during the course of human history and climactically in the person of Jesus, the Word and Son. At other times, however, the discourse is strictly philosophical in character, although further designed to clarify or advance the work of theological reflection, somewhat as complex mathematical elucidations advance the understanding of questions in theoretical physics. There are long stretches of the second section of the second part of the *Summa*, in which Thomas is filling out the portrait of the ideal man. This is moral philosophy that finds a place here because the subject of redemption is a man before he is a Christian and does not cease to owe allegiance to what is authentically human when he is called to the Christian life. To be valid, these philosophical assertions must be grounded, not on authority, but on the facts of common experience as interpreted by the natural human intelligence. For outside theology, Thomas remarked on one occasion, the argument from authority is the weakest possible one (*S. Th.*, I, a. 1, a. 8, ad 2). In his commentary on Aristotle's *De Coelo* he further observes that the purpose of philosophy is not to know the opinions of men but the truth of the matter (*In lib. De Coelo et Mundo*, b. 1, lect. 22, n. 8). Yet one should add that Thomas would also have said that theology too deals with facts—with the divine interventions in human history to whose meaning faith gives access.

The methods of philosophy and theology are, then, different and Thomas himself distinguished them clearly. In the monograph written in 1270 to criticize the Averroistic doctrine of a single intellect shared by all men, he remarks explicitly that he is doing philosophy, not theology.[17] Since he did both, it is possible to extract a philosophy from his theological writings. One of the debated questions among twentieth-century Thomists has dealt with the question of how the autonomy of the philosophy thus extracted is to be understood. Some would see it as Christian only in the sense of harmoniously coexisting with the Christian outlook. Others insist that this philosophical dimension of Thomas' thought, though truly philosophical because it derives from contact with experience and not from faith, has nonetheless been intrinsically influenced by that faith. Revelation has, for instance, sometimes raised questions for philosophical consideration that might otherwise have been overlooked. The possession of both a divine and human nature by the one person, Jesus, has stimulated a study of the metaphysical constituents of personality. Moreover, even when doing philosophy the Christian who wishes to remain in the Thomistic tradition ought, according to some Thomists, to follow that theological ordering of topics found in the *Summa*. That is to say, he should begin with the divine and move then to a study of the universe of men and things. This contention is rejected by other thinkers who judge it incompatible with the philosophical approach that must commence with man himself. Howsoever this subtle debate is resolved, what should be noted here is that Thomas' intellectual achievement is itself a prime example of the distinctive harmonizing of the religious and the secular within a single work and that it is accomplished not by denying the intrinsic value of philosophy but by ordering it finally to the work of theology.

A HIGH NOON OF LEARNING

This question of Thomas' philosophy and its Greek sources turns our attention to the last of the thirteenth-century characteristics that we should like to underscore —the confident vitality of its intellectual life. It was an age marked by a creative enthusiasm for learning and a robust but measured confidence in the possibilities of human intelligence. Naturally enough, this feature of the mental climate was most perceptible in university circles.

In the thirteenth century everyone received an education. It could scarcely have been otherwise, for no society regenerates itself except by transmitting its way of life to the rising generation, and were it not to educate a sizable portion of the educable, it would perish. But

education, of course, is not synonymous with book learning or erudition, and in the Middle Ages the majority
were not literate. For as Joan Evans points out, medieval
education aimed to prepare people for their adult functions in society.[18] So the peasant children learned the
skills of farmer or housewife; the apprentices mastered
the appropriate techniques of their craft; the nobility acquired the arts of a feudal administrator or chatelaine;
and bright boys destined for civil or ecclesiastical service
went to the university. Indeed, they went in relatively
large numbers. Reliable statistics are scarce because the
figures of the contemporary chroniclers are considered
dubious. But even if there were not tens of thousands at
Paris when Thomas taught there, modern historians
judge it not unlikely that there were five to seven thousand students.[19] It is true that they came from all over
Europe, but it is also true that Paris was not the only
university. In France alone there were Orléans, Angers,
and Toulouse, and elsewhere such large centers as Oxford,
Cambridge, and Bologna. In modern times numbers of
this sort would not be found at Paris or in any American
or English university until recent decades of the twentieth century. We may conclude that a sizable percentage
of the eligible males of the High Middle Ages spent some
time at a university.

Surely not all these students were seriously interested
in ideas. Many must have had practical, vocational ob-
jectives in mind, and some were dilettantes. But for those
who had, as Thomas did, the time and aptitude for a
life of learning, the thirteenth century was a good age
to be alive. It was one of those moments when a sweeping
new perspective on reality suddenly shakes the consciousness of the intellectual world so as to energize and elate
it. For during Thomas' lifetime Western Europe came
into possession of the full Aristotelian *corpus* after having
known only part of his logic. We may compress centuries
of intellectual history into a few sentences and recall that

Plato rather than Aristotle was the master of classical philosophy until the fall of Rome—not Platonism in itself but in the neo-Platonic synthesis or fused with Stoic elements. Aristotle with his empiricism, his interest in science and in the visible world investigable not only by metaphysics but by biology, physics, politics, and ethics for a vast unified synthesis, was not congenial to those who preferred philosophy to be a kind of religion and found it so in Plotinus. The early Middle Ages liked all it knew of Aristotle, which was some of the *Organon* studied in Latin translation as the pith of the discipline known as Dialectic. In the thirteenth century the rest of Aristotle became available through two channels. From Moorish Spain and the Saracen elements in Sicily, the Aristotelian treatises percolated through Latin versions of the great Arabic commentaries, particularly those of Averroes (Ibn Rushd) of Cordova (1126–1198). After the Fourth Crusade had in 1204 obligingly conquered Christian Constantinople rather than the fortresses of Islam, there was access to the original Greek text of Aristotle. Thomas, as we noted, did not himself read Greek, but his Flemish colleague, William of Moerbeke, made literal translations for him.

Why should he have wanted them? Because as a professional theologian Aquinas used philosophical findings as a tool for penetrating the great themes, or mysteries, of the biblical faith cherished by the Christian community. Heretofore the philosophy principally employed for this work of understanding, elaboration, and defense of Christian belief had been neo-Platonism as transmuted by the genius of St. Augustine and bequeathed to the following millennium. Thomas did not neglect this patrimony. He assimilated it just as he did much of Plato. His writings contain hundreds of references to Plato and the Platonists, and contemporary scholars have concluded that Aquinas' use of Platonic and neo-Platonic insights is more extensive and significant than was once recognized. But that recognition was delayed because it is otherwise so evident that Thomas, generally speaking, used Aristotelian philosophy in the work of theological speculation where Augustine had used neo-Platonism. He did so, he remarked in the *Summa* when contrasting the noetics of Plato and Aristotle, because our experience corroborates the Aristotelian analysis (S. *Th.*, I, q. 88, a. 1, c.). His Franciscan contemporaries did not think so and continued the Augustinian philosophical tradition, which could seem, at first glance, more sympathetic to the Christian world view. For as A. E. Taylor once nicely put it, if the Gospel had been announced to the great Greek philosophers, it would have been Plato with his vision of a reality beyond this visible world who would have seemed most likely to respond and not Aristotle, the biologist and physicist, so thoroughly at home in that very world.

What Thomas and his former teacher, Albert the Great, aimed at was, therefore, both new and bold. In theologizing, Aquinas would use not only Aristotelian logic but the integrated view of cosmos, man, and morals inspired by Aristotle's physics, metaphysics, and ethics. Whatever in this philosophy was itself reasonable, and therefore necessarily compatible with Christianity, Thomas adopted and often refined and developed. What was clearly incompatible with Christianity, like Aristotle's doctrine of the eternity of the world, he would reject. What was inchoate in Aristotle, he would interpret in a sense not anti-Christian. What needed to be added, like a defense of the immortality of the human soul, he would add without trying to claim Aristotle for it. But to do this last he had to effect what Gilson calls a metamorphosis of Aristotle's principles.[20]

What made this whole business doubly hard to justify in the eyes of the traditionalists was the vocal presence on the academic scene of quite another interpretation of Aristotle. This latter is called "Latin Averroism." "Latin," because it is a question of its defense by such men in Latin-speaking Western Europe as the Flemish priest, Siger of Brabant, who was teaching at Paris in the 1260s —and who also joined Aquinas as one of the twelve lights in Dante's vision of Paradise. "Averroism," because it is a question of Aristotle as seen through the Moorish philosopher's commentaries. Averroes was a figure so compelling that Thomas, like many medieval writers, called him simply *the* commentator, just as Aristotle was *the* philosopher. But where Aquinas would, on occasion, transform Aristotle, Averroes adhered to what the philosopher said, or developed his ideas within the logic of the Aristotelian system. This meant that Averroes argued against individual freedom and immortality; denied divine providence; asserted that the world was eternal; and held that there is but a single intellect in which all men share. Since these positions were hopelessly opposed to Christian teaching, some Latin Averroists who were much impressed by them concluded that there were two kinds of truth, so that a proposition could be true in philosophy but false in theology.

In the quarrel joined over this issue Thomas Aquinas occupied the kind of center position that is hardest to defend. For on the one hand, he had to maintain against Siger that Averroes, as Thomas said, really *perverted* Aristotle's thought in these instances (*De Unitate Intellectus contra Averroistas*, c. 1). On the other hand, Thomas had to argue against the Augustinians that his own brand of Aristotelianism was very unlike Siger's and quite in accord with Christian belief. But up to the time of his death he had not persuaded everyone of this position. In 1277 the Bishop of Paris condemned a trunkload of opinions descending from Aristotle in some way or other, and several of Thomas' own theses were among them. Aristotle, in short, was still a symbol of advanced thinking. Later on Aristotelianism would itself harden into a received doctrine that conserved rather than stimulated.

This was, as Ernest Barker has noted, an ironic and tragic betrayal of Aristotle's honestly empirical spirit. Nevertheless, it happened, and so scientific progress required criticism of Aristotelian science. But the precedent for such criticism had already been provided by the sort of selective approach to Aristotle that Thomas personified.[21]

It is sometimes said nowadays that Pierre Teilhard de Chardin stands to modern intellectual movements somewhat as Thomas Aquinas did to those of the thirteenth century. Perhaps comparisons of this sort are not very instructive even when they are plausible. But if narrowed down enough, they may have some use. For Teilhard also occupied a middle position in the matter of a particular cosmological perspective. He hoped to persuade agnostics that the concept of an evolving universe does not preclude finality or design. Indeed, he believed that the long series of evolutionary transformations displayed a definite direction and line of advance. Hence he also wanted to persuade theologians that the evolutionary vision of the cosmos harmonizes with and enriches the Christian view of things. This was not unlike the work of assimilation done for Aristotelian science and theory by Thomas in the thirteenth century. And the parallel points up the theme we want to accent here—that Thomas' day was one of intellectual excitement and challenge for the Christian thinker, much as our own is now.

What distinguished Thomas' response to this sort of challenge was his confidence in the range and power of philosophical thought. This is not to say either that his overall estimate of man's rationality was more inflated than ours or that he ignored the limitations of reason and the demonic power of the irrational. He expected rather less than we do from the practical exercise of intelligence and rather more from its speculative use. In his commentary on the sixth book of the *Nicomachean Ethics* Thomas expounded Aristotle's distinction between two modes or manners of intelligent action, neither of which can simply be reduced to the other. The practical kind of activity shows itself in the arts and technology as well as in scientific experimentation. In all such cases we deliberate about the means for achieving a particular goal or producing a particular effect and then convert our decision into action. The "truth" of our deliberations, Thomas held, depends upon whether or not the means chosen did in fact achieve the end or produce the desired effect. The result is to be measured by the degree to which it fulfills our intention (*S. Th.*, I-II, q. 57, a. 5, ad 3, and *De Ver.*, q. 1, a. 2). The primitive hunter wandering through the forest wonders if a log on the bank is long enough and strong enough to bridge the stream. He tries it out, and, if he actually gets across, his hypothesis has been confirmed. This pragmatic intelligence is also applied to problems in human relationships. But since the moral dimension is intrinsic to such questions, the action taken in their regard cannot properly be called "true" unless it is also ethical—or, as Thomas would say, "conformed to right appetite."

Aristotle and Aquinas, however, also held that we can arrive at certain truths that are not the issue of practical action nor expressed in operational formulae. Authentic knowledge of this sort is acquired by an active but non-pragmatic functioning of intelligence. This insightful or meditative exercise of reason shows itself as a prehensive power that can penetrate to a true, though hardly an exhaustive, understanding of things as they really are. We can recognize an object as having the appearance of a chair, although we cannot know whether it is comfortable or not until we try it out. This contemplative power is manifested in a simple, fleeting way every time we get the point of a joke and, more importantly, in the intuitions of the scientist and artist or the insightful grasp of ethical norms.

One might say that a John Dewey effectively appreciated the instrumental function of intelligence while disallowing Aristotle's *nous theoretikos,* the power for truth whose criterion is other than that of success in action. (In fact, however, Dewey was a subtle and creative contemplator as all famous philosophers have been.) Thomas, on the other hand, recognized the role of the pragmatic intelligence but spent little time on it. Perhaps he would have said that it is the business of administrators to concern themselves with large practical affairs and the setting up of institutions "useful for the human community" (*S. Th.,* I-II, q. 97, a. 1, c.). Against Marx's celebrated dictum he would have urged that the philosopher's distinctive task is precisely to understand the world rather than to change it.

On balance, though, it is likely that Thomas' optimism about speculative thinking was not as great as some of our contemporaries' hopes for pragmatic thinking. The pragmatic outlook, nourished by the successes of science and technology, is indeed valuable because it both inspires and arms men for the kind of action that seizes events and orders them toward ever more humane ends. But in its most exuberant spokesmen it is volitalized into a utopianism promising salvation through scientific rationality. St. Thomas never claimed as much for reason. He is confident, to be sure, that the existence of God can be demonstrated, and this strikes many today as excessive. Yet Thomas appraises quite coolly the reach of thought in this very matter. He knows that we have no immediate knowledge of God and that we are always in danger of identifying our conceptual constructs, howsoever sophisticated, with the Divine. "We cannot grasp what God is," said Thomas, "but what he is not and how other things stand to Him" (*CG,* I, c. 30). From our experience of this world, we can argue to God's existence, but we cannot understand that existence and must speak of God obscurely and by analogy (*ibid.* and *S. Th.,* I, q. 3, a. 4, ad 2). Thus it happens, as Thomas points out, that a man attains more effectively to God by loving Him than by thinking about Him. For the impulse of love reaches directly to the Beloved albeit in darkness.

If Thomas would, then, be surprised at all we propose and manage to do through control of our natural environment, we are likely to be surprised at all he proposed and managed to do by confident speculative power. For in the *Summa Theologiae* he synthesizes in a panoramic vision all his thought about God and man and the universe. The synthesis itself may have lost its appeal, but it remains a serene and bold affirmation of the nobility and uses of reason.

◇ NOTES ◇

1. This is pointed out by Robert P. Goodwin in his introduction to *Selected Writings of St. Thomas Aquinas* (Indianapolis: Bobbs-Merrill, 1965), p. xii.
2. The factual details of St. Thomas Aquinas' life are drawn almost entirely from Angelus Walz, O.P., *Saint Thomas Aquinas: A Biographical Study,* trans. Sebastian Bullough, O.P. (Westminster, Md.: Newman Press, 1951). Where dates are a matter of dispute, Father Walz's choices are followed. Vernon Bourke's *Aquinas' Search for Wisdom* (Milwaukee: Bruce, 1965) is a very helpful study, which gathers up what is known about Thomas' life and also summarizes his work and the main lines of his thought.
3. In the Introduction to a French translation of Book I of the *Summa contra Gentiles* (Paris: P. Lethielleux, 1961), A. Gauthier makes several points about St. Thomas' intentions in this work: (1) The title appears to have been given to it by a "badly inspired" secretary rather than by Thomas himself. (2) This title is inexact because the treatise is not really a *Summa* that would be a manual for beginners covering in condensed

fashion all the chief theological topics—a summary summation, so to speak. The *Contra Gentiles* is more properly to be called a *Liber,* or book discussing selected topics for a sophisticated reader. (3) The traditional story that Aquinas designed the *Contra Gentiles* as a handbook for young Dominican missionaries to the Spanish Moors is a legend without foundation. See pp. 60–90. Father Eschmann, however, writing in 1956, considered that tradition "still sound." See I. T. Eschmann, O.P., "A Catalogue of St. Thomas's Works," in Etienne Gilson, *The Christian Philosophy of St. Thomas Aquinas,* trans. L. K. Shook, C.S.B. (New York: Random House, 1956), p. 385.

4. Henri Pirenne, *A History of Europe from the Invasions to the XVI Century,* trans. Bernard Miall (New York: Norton, 1939), p. 311.

5. Ernst Kantorowicz, *Frederick the Second 1194–1250,* trans. E. O. Lorimer (New York: Frederick Ungar, 1957), p. 270.

6. Pirenne, *op. cit.,* p. 291.

7. See Friedrich Heer, *The Medieval World: Europe 1100–1350,* trans. Janet Sondheimer (Cleveland: World, 1962), p. 106.

8. Philip Hughes, *A History of the Church: An Introductory Study* (New York: Sheed and Ward, 1935), Vol. II, p. 408; and Brian Tierney, *The Crisis of Church and State 1050–1300* (Englewood Cliffs, N.J.: Prentice-Hall, 1964), pp. 97–101, 116–119.

9. Quoted by Joan Evans, *Life in Medieval France* (London: Oxford University Press, 1925), p. 174.

10. John T. Noonan, Jr., *The Scholastic Analysis of Usury* (Cambridge: Harvard University Press, 1957), pp. 31, 42.

11. Ernst Troeltsch, *The Social Teaching of the Christian Churches,* trans. Olive Wyon (New York: Harper Torchbooks, Harper & Row, 1960), Vol. I, p. 303. The original German edition of this work appeared in 1911, and the English translation was first published in 1931. See also Philip Arthur Micklem, *The Secular and the*

Sacred: An Enquiry into the Principles of a Christian Civilization (London: Hodder and Stoughton, 1948), p. 157.

12. See Hughes, *op. cit.*, p. 408, and John Neville Figgis, *Political Thought from Gerson to Grotius 1414–1625* (New York: Harper & Row, 1960), p. 5. This is a reprinting of a work that first appeared in 1907.

13. Quoted in Harvey Gates Townsend, *Philosophical Ideas in the United States* (New York: American Book, 1934), p. 58.

14. See Alfons Auer, "The Changing Character of the Christian Understanding of the World," in Alfons Auer, *et al.*, *The Christian and the World: Readings in Theology* (New York: P. J. Kenedy and Sons, 1965), p. 15; and Johannes B. Metz, "A Believer's Look at the World—A Christian Standpoint in the Secularized World of Today," in *ibid.*, p. 70.

15. M.-D. Chenu, O.P., "Consecratio Mundi," in *ibid.*, p. 170.

16. "Pastoral Constitution on the Church in the Modern World," in *Documents of Vatican II* (Guild-America-Association Presses, 1966), p. 233, n. 36 of the document.

17. "Haec igitur sunt quae . . . conscripsimus, non per documenta fidei, sed per ipsorum philosophorum rationes." *De Unitate Intellectus contra Averroistas*, c. 5. This is from the final paragraph of the work.

18. Evans, *op. cit.*, p. 149.

19. Lowrie J. Daly, S.J., *The Medieval University: 1200–1400* (New York: Sheed and Ward, 1961), pp. 208–210.

20. Etienne Gilson, *History of Christian Philosophy in the Middle Ages* (New York: Random House, 1955), p. 365.

21. On medieval criticism of Aristotle see A. C. Crombie, *Augustine to Galileo: The History of Science A.D. 400–1650* (London: Falcon Press, 1952), pp. 212–273.

·III·
Thomistic Themes for a Philosophy of Education

Philosophy of education, which is an effort to relate a generalized discussion of the aims, curricula, methods, and agencies of formal schooling to a philosophy of life and value, flourishes so notably in the United States as almost to seem an American invention like the motel. This may be partly due to the unparalleled size of our educational establishment and to our hopeful faith in what it can accomplish. Our spacious conception of education is, in fact, suggested by the way we use the term. For it is a commonplace among philologists that a people's distinctive use of words points to a distinctive way of seeing the world. Now Americans have not usually drawn a distinction between "instruction," the chief business of the school, and the wider, if vaguer, concept of "education" thought of primarily as the development of character and personality. This distinction between *enseignement* and *éducation*, between *Erziehung* and *Bildung*, is well established elsewhere but has not become an American usage, probably because it has not seemed to Americans that these two aspects should or can be separated. This view may have its bad effects. Some people think it accounts for the schools' failure, particularly in higher education, to fulfill their specific intellectual function as well as they might because they are confused about their role.[1] However that may be, at least the theorists among us have had their attention directed steadily toward a richer and more stimulating conception of education than that merely of instruction.

CONCEPTS OF "EDUCATION" AND "LEARNING" IN THOMISM

St. Thomas Aquinas, however, did make a distinction between *educatio* and *disciplina*. He used the former term very rarely but once defined it in the *Commentary on the Sentences* as "the advancement of the child to the state of specifically human excellence, that is to say, to the state of virtue" (Bk. IV, dist. 26, q. 1, a. 1). *Disciplina*, on the other hand, appears somewhat more often. It is best, if awkwardly, translated as "learning-by-being-taught" as distinguished from *inventio*, or "learning-by-oneself." The teaching that *disciplina* connotes, however, is instruction in quite a sharply defined sense. It is verified when one person teaches another a "science" like mathematics, physics, or logic in which there is a firmly articulated descent of particular conclusions from self-evident premises that have themselves usually been grasped by a kind of intuition from experience. For *scientia*, in its turn, is understood by Aquinas as "the ability to demonstrate conclusions from principles" (*S. Th.*, I-II,

q. 57, a. 2, ad 1).[2] It is only where this sort of learning product is concerned that a man can really be said to teach someone else. He does this if he can so draw upon his own learning experiences as to help others arrive at the necessary insight into principles and then trace the logical procession of various conclusions from them.

It is worth noting that Thomas shared Aristotle's skepticism about Plato's thesis that moral virtue could, strictly speaking, be taught. In the geometry class, to use Aquinas' stock example, the students are indeed taught when they are brought to see for themselves that two parallel lines can never meet in Euclid's universe. The teacher can, therefore, be called an instrumental and secondary cause of the student's learning since he expedites the essential activity of the pupil's own powers, which are the chief and indispensable cause (*De Ver.*, q. 11, a. 1, c.). But while the teacher might help that same student come to some notion of the nature and value of truthfulness, that would hardly guarantee his being honest. So when Thomas spoke on one occasion of moral education, he used the verb *assuescere* rather than *docere*. The best one can hope to do, he implied, is to accustom young people to acting virtuously so that they may develop good habits through the exercise of their own free action (*In lib. Eth.*, b. II, lect. 1).

But even what Thomas has to say about *disciplinae*, these intellectual learnings that can be aided by instruction, forms only a tiny and somewhat peripheral feature of his vast systematic landscape, so that concentrating upon his references to education is rather like studying Churchill under the formality of a painter. This Thomistic synthesis is worked out in a library of writings, which can be classified according to a threefold division. There are the commentaries on other authors: the Scriptures, Aristotle and two early Christian writers, Boethius and the pseudo-Dionysius. There are the three great theological syntheses: the *Commentary on the Sentences*,

the *Summa contra Gentiles,* and the *Summa Theologiae.*
Finally, there is a shelf of monographs and short treatises
that take up a variety of specific theological and philosophical issues. These include the *Academic Disputations* and the *Quodlibet Questions,* which grew out of
certain formal and public academic exercises at Paris, as
well as some thirty or more smaller essays called *opuscula.*

Thomas was accustomed to introduce reflections on
one topic while professedly treating of another, since he
was always interested in perceiving relationships among
ideas. Consequently, he sometimes illustrated or applied
a theological or philosophical position by a brief reference
to education.[3] This sort of digression happens quite
naturally in his commentary on Aristotle's *Ethics,* and if
Thomas had completed the commentary he started on
the *Politics,* the materials of the seventh and eighth
books would have occasioned many more observations
about education. But as it is, only in the eleventh of the
Quaestiones Disputatae de Veritate, a short discussion
sometimes called *De Magistro* (On the Teacher), and in
the corresponding passages in the *Summa Theologiae,*
does Thomas examine strictly pedagogical questions at
any length. In these places he proposes an illuminating
philosophical analysis of *disciplina* or "learning-through-
instruction." Of course, there is a good deal more to the
concrete teaching situation than this. Still, we should
not underestimate the *De Magistro,* for it is a highly
nourishing concentrate from which more than one essay
on education has been brewed, even though its recommendations are not yet universally honored. For Thomas
demonstrates metaphysically that learning is a process
of growth brought about primarily by the learner's own
activity. This provides firm support for pedagogies designed to make students mainly responsible for their own
learning so that they may more surely develop into persons capable of independent intellectual inquiry and
evolution. The teacher who hopes to expedite this process

is advised by Aquinas, who anticipates Rousseau, to follow nature—that is, the methods men use when they
learn on their own. We shall touch again on these themes
from the *De Magistro* in some paragraphs below on
teaching.

The oblique comments on education that Thomas
sprinkles elsewhere in his writings are sensible but rather
rudimentary. It is sometimes said that the enormous second section of the second part of the *Summa Theologiae*
can be regarded as an educational treatise of sorts since it
deals with the moral life, with the nature and the achievement of ethical self-realization, which is, after all, the
ultimate concern of education. But this is not what is
usually meant today by "philosophy of education." The
substance of the *Secunda Secundae* is a detailed study of
the Christian ethic and not an essay in educational theory.
True enough, it is fleshed out with a wealth of examples,
applications, and comments that illustrate the argument
and prove that Thomas was a sharp observer of human
nature. But these marginal notes cannot be compared
with the detailed analyses of contemporary personality
theory, social psychology, and cultural anthropology.
Even run-of-the-mill textbooks in educational psychology
contain more sophisticated materials on human behavior
than we can expect to find in the work of a medieval
theological moralist.

It is not, then, to the passages treating explicitly of
education that we ought to look if we want to sketch out
the elements of Thomas' thought that have the greatest
significance for educational theory. It is rather certain
nuclear theological and philosophical themes that are
most meaningful—especially if education is taken in that
broader sense that Americans find congenial. This is not
to say that Thomas made explicit the various connections
between his thought and school practice or that the applications themselves will appeal to everyone. What is
meant is that the reflections of a philosopher or the-

ologian on man and the world will have implications for education and that these will be more or less specific depending upon how interested he was in drawing them out. In Dewey's small classic, *The School and Society*, manual work projects are strongly recommended for the elementary school. But one will fully understand why Dewey wanted children to have a garden, a carpenter shop, or a loom only in light of his epistemology and metaphysics. For these activities are encouraged precisely because they develop certain crucial human excellences: problem-solving thinking and friendly cooperativeness. These, in turn, are desirable dispositions, Dewey thought, because they are indispensable tools that men must employ in their evolving natural and social environments where critical options can only be resolved pragmatically and the human family can only advance through fraternal collaboration.

The student of educational theory is well advised, therefore, to turn his attention to what Thomas has to say about the nature of man and his life in this universe, since from this ground fruitful recommendations for education might conceivably emerge whether or not Thomas himself cultivated them. Whoever does embark upon this enterprise will find, as we have remarked, a complex texture in which philosophical ideas are intermingled with theological ones. Thomas did not bother to emphasize the distinction between these two strands, since it was the unitary character of truth that most impressed him. His distinctive intellectual achievement, in fact, is to have synthesized the religious and the secular dimensions of his thought without impoverishing the character of either. He knew when he was philosophizing and when he was theologizing, and we can separate the elements drawn from revelation from those based on experience.

One more caution bears repeating. At a level of high generalization it is possible to say that Thomas' philosophy of man, like that of all the medieval scholastics, is continuous with the Platonic-Aristotelian tradition, which appealed to Christian theologians as the tradition of Democritus or the Sophists could not. Furthermore, it is also true that Thomas sided with Aristotle rather than with Plato at certain decisive junctures. Plato, according to Aquinas, regarded man as essentially a mind—*homo sit ipse intellectus* (*S. Th.*, I, q. 76, a. 2, c.)—not as a natural composite of soul and body but as a soul using a body (*CG*, b. II, c. 57). This view, whether an accurate transcription of Platonism or not, was as unacceptable to Thomas as to Aristotle. But at the same time, Aquinas' portrait of man as an incarnate spirit possessing the essential unity of an animated body could hardly have been recognized by Aristotle as his own. For Aristotelianism did not envision a substantial form that would continue to exist after the composition that it helped constitute had deteriorated. What Thomas did here was quietly to effect one of his transformations and to argue on philosophical grounds that the human soul, this substantial form that is the principle whereby a man exists, eats, walks, feels, and thinks, does remain in existence even after the body has been corrupted (*S. Th.*, I, q. 76, a. 1, c. and ad 5).

In this view, man is more than a purely material organization, howsoever complex. He is rather a unique composition of body and consciousness, a "Spirit in the World," to use the epigrammatic title of Karl Rahner's book, which was itself a prolonged reflection upon the epistemology associated with this common scholastic tenet. For his part, Thomas Aquinas was not much given to minting quotable maxims, but on occasion he did sum up this central thesis about man in a striking phrase. Man is unique, he wrote, because he is composed of a corporeal and a spiritual substance and is, therefore, set between two worlds with his soul situated on the boundary between heaven and earth. It will be useful to stop a while over this notion and its implications for education.

"SPIRIT IN THE WORLD"

Man's thinking, said Thomas in the *Summa Theologiae,* is nobler than any of the activities he shares with the infrahuman world (*S. Th.*, I, q. 92, a. 1, c.). The mind ranks ahead of everything else in the human make-up since all the other powers, particularly the senses, are designed for the service of the intelligence (*S. Th.*, I, q. 76, a. 2, c.). This is a definite enough position but not one that wins universal consent. Karl Marx would have agreed with it, for as his son-in-law, Paul Lafargue, said of him, "Thinking was his supreme enjoyment. I have often heard him quote from Hegel, the master of the philosophy of his youthful days, the saying: 'Even the criminal thought of a scoundrel is grander and more sublime than the wonders of the heavens.' " [4]

There are contemporary thinkers, however, who would insist that man's sexuality is more important than his intellectuality. There are others who indignantly see in this thesis of the pre-eminence of intelligence an insufferable attempt to dissociate man from the animal part of his nature and his community with bird and beast. They judge the attempt to be as wrong-headed as it is snobbish. For do not men, in fact, often act with cruel irrationality, and do not the brutes often manifest remarkable patterns of knowledge and cooperation?—although one must concede that they have never invented speech, or tools, or culture.

There is no space nor need here for involvement in this particular discussion. It is necessary to point out, though, that Thomas was aware of the qualifications that must be made. He knew of the wide range of instinctual behavior and sensation among animals from the immobile mussel at one end of the spectrum to the sagacious bees, spiders, and hunting dogs at the other (*CG*, b. II, c. 68 and *S. Th.*, I-II, q. 13, a. 2, ad 3). He also knew that men, more often than not, choose to act in accordance with sensory attractions rather than with reason's judgments (*S. Th.*, I, q. 49, a. 3, ad 5). What he affirmed, however, was his conviction that man is most himself when he is most rational and that this is his distinctive mark. The uniqueness of the human condition cannot be located in such qualities as extension, sensation, and sexuality, which man shares with the lower animals even though all these are essential parts of his nature and either necessary or influential for thought.

Should someone equate rationality with goodness and then go on to object that reason can scarcely be central in men, seeing that they frequently behave worse than the beasts, Thomas would reply that only intelligent beings are even capable of the morally right or wrong, although reason and virtue are not identical. Without the ability to recognize and evaluate contrasting alternatives, there can be no such thing as a free choice between good and evil or between the greater and lesser good and hence, no morality. Scholastics like Aquinas were, in fact, led to affirm this pre-eminence of intellectuality because of the characteristics they observed in the activities we call intelligent. The two marks that particularly stood out may be called "self-consciousness" and "transcendence." These are not terms employed by St. Thomas, but we choose them precisely because in contemporary philosophical and theological writings they are often used to designate aspects of the human condition about which Thomas had a good deal to say.

In the *Summa contra Gentiles* Aquinas contrasts succinctly the levels of plant, animal, and intellectual activity and concludes that the highest grade of life is the intellectual, since it manifests the greatest degree of knowledge and self-movement (*CG*, b. IV, c. 11). For a man can be aware of himself. He can reflect upon his actions and in the very act of knowing an object also know himself, the conscious subject, and know that he knows. This means, as we would put it today, that he is able to say "I," since he can predicate his activity of himself. That is part of what it means to be a person, and it points to a spiritual constituent in personality, since sheer matter has not this capacity for bending wholly back upon itself in a complete reflection, just as no knife can cut itself.

The second nuclear function of intelligence is its power to release man from complete imprisonment in the realm of material facts. The potentiality and reach of the rational function make men capable of a certain transcendence of nature's determinism. In the north woods, as winter approaches, the birds go south and the bears crawl into caves. But the citizens of Duluth continue about their business and dress for evening parties although the thermometer has dropped far below zero. The practical intelligence, howsoever philosophers may conceive it, has made it possible for these people to transcend both an intractably hostile environment and the grooves of a sheerly instinctive conformity to its conditions.

Of course, this transcendence is not total and men are not angels. Aquinas sees mankind as part of a great chain of being that extends from the geosphere up through the angelic orders of pure spirits. In his philosophy, therefore, man is indeed immanent and firmly rooted in this world; not divorced from that context nor a stranger there. At the same time, since human intelligence has dramatically proven itself a most effective tool for controlling and transforming this earthly environment, men are to some degree independent of the natural elements. There is a passage in the seventh of the *Quodlibet Questions* that is sometimes called *De Opere*

Manuali—On Manual Work. Thomas is out to show here that manual work is connatural to man and not simply a penalty for sin. He argues in quite an instrumental and even evolutionary fashion to point up the way intelligence effects a mastery over, and thereby a transcendence of, the primeval situation. Aquinas writes:

> As is clear from the very structure of his body man has a natural orientation to manual work. For this reason it is said in Job 5:7: "Man was born to labor and the bird was born to fly." Nature has adequately provided all the other animals with whatever they require in the way of food, weapons, and covering for the maintenance of life. Man is not thus equipped because he is gifted with intelligence wherewith to supply himself with these things. Consequently, in their place, man has hands which are adapted to fashioning all sorts of products answering to his mental conceptions (Quodlibet VII, a. 17, c. See also S. Th., I-II, q. 95, a. 1, c.).

Or as Thomas put it in his commentary on one of the Aristotelian treatises in Logic, the *De Interpretatione* (or *Peri Hermeneias*), because men are not limited to sense knowledge, as beasts are, they can surmount the "here" and "now" and attend to what is ahead of them in the future or far off from them in place (*In lib. Peri Her.*, b. I, lect. 2).

From all this one can see that for Thomas, as for the scholastic tradition generally, man's cognitive interaction with the encompassing world is to be thought of as pluralistic. Aquinas recognized two natural sources of knowledge. Intelligence and the whole complex of senses, which include sight, hearing, and touch, are the proper endowments of nature; and their fruits are distinguished from the knowledge obtained by acceptance of divine revelation. But in this natural approach to reality one is never, according to Thomas' hypothesis, either simply thinking or merely sensing. The two functions are unified in the operation of a distinctively human way of knowing. And just as sensation is not the only kind of cognitive experience, so intellection is not a matter of shuffling and regrouping sense images. The Thomistic analysis of knowledge argues that intellection penetrates more deeply than the senses are capable of doing into the sense data in order to grasp intelligible or transensible aspects of reality embedded or somehow implied in these data but beyond the reach of the senses (*S. Th.*, I, q. 78, a. 4, ad 4).

Indeed, if we reflect upon our own psychic life, we notice these two sorts of phenomena. We are aware, on the one hand, of an immediate contact with things and persons about us through our senses: We feel the summer heat, catch a fragrance, hear voices, taste honey, and are dazzled by color. On the other hand, we are also aware that we abstract from our experience to talk about this or that as characteristic of men or animals, of French children or of Chinese women. We say that a true appreciation of freedom demands thus-and-so, or that these are the principles of art, or that good government calls for such-and-such a balance of forces. This power of generalizing from experience is "mind," which, said Aquinas, "cannot directly attain to singular things" (*In lib. Peri Her.*, b. I, lect. 14).

In Aquinas' anthropology one of the most brilliant and subtle metaphysical excursions is designed to explain how this intellectual knowledge arises out of the interpenetrating action of sense and intelligence. Any good summary of Thomistic psychology will sketch for the reader the outlines of this theory, which is still being debated and refined by specialists, although, to tell the truth, it is not the sort of problem that much attracts the generality of contemporary philosophers. It was devised, as we have noted, to interpret facts of ordinary experience which for Thomas pointed to the existence of two levels of knowing. He once remarked, in this connection, that brute animals are only pleased by sensible objects connected with food or sex, whereas man can enjoy for itself the beauty of the sensible world (S. Th., I, q. 91, a. 3, ad 3). Because the senses are bodily powers they unite us directly with individual things of a material sort—the color and scent of this rose. The intelligence, in turn, does what the senses cannot do: It conceptualizes this experience. As we touch or smell or see the rose, we form a notion that can be predicated of many roses, so that whenever we meet that flower again we can truly recognize its family. This is possible, Aquinas thought, because in the process of understanding, a universal aspect has been liberated from the concrete materiality, which, in the real as distinguished from the intentional order, ties it down to one or other particular. Yet this process, culminating in the judgment where truth is formally achieved, necessarily begins with sense awareness even though it has a certain freedom from it (S. Th., I, q. 84, a. 7, c.). Sense experience is therefore indispensable for human growth in and through knowledge, and we shall return to this point when we summarize below what Thomas has to say about teaching.

Here, however, we want to underline a further dimension of that transcendence that characterizes man in his thinking. Looked at in itself, this thinking is a limited activity. It depends, for instance, upon sensory contact with the material world. Our minds do not attain directly and intuitively either to God or to individual material beings, although we can reason to the existence of the former and sense the latter.* But from another point of

* Duns Scotus (1265/66–1308), who was a generation or two younger than Thomas, was distinctive in the thirteenth century for holding that we do have a direct intellection of the individual. A modern writer, who is a Franciscan like Scotus, suggests rather darkly that a depreciation of the individual in favor of the collective, as well as the brutalities of medieval penal practice, may be traced to the doctrine that the mind does not directly know individuals. See Alan Keenan, O.F.M., "Duns Scotus and the Renewal," *The Month*, New Series XXXVI (Novem-

view the human mind appears to be limitless. At least our appetite for knowledge has a kind of infinity since it is not satiated by knowing any one finite object or a multitude of them. This dynamism toward unlimited knowledge, toward knowing more things or knowing more about those we have met, is intelligence itself. Moreover, it constitutes us as open not only to material things with which we interact but even to the infinite plenitude of being we name God. And this in three ways. We can, for one thing, raise the question of God and wish to know its answer. In addition, Thomas was persuaded that one might argue to God's existence by reflection upon certain facts of experience that require this conclusion if they are to be ultimately intelligible. He sketched the outline of such argumentation in the celebrated fivefold way of the *Summa*. But he also saw this human appetite for knowledge as itself a natural tendency toward, or openness to, God. For just as our desire for a perfect, unlimited happiness is the ground for our response to the partial goodness found in any particular thing, so we respond to the intelligibility of limited beings because our mind is ordered to the infinitely intelligible that is infinite existence.

Of course, we do not necessarily recognize the character of this dynamism although it is there for discovery by introspection. And even when one has recognized the tendency and affirmed, either by the religious assent of faith or by philosophical reasoning, that God is not

---

ber, 1966), 256–257. But this seems to credit a technical philosophical question with undue influence upon the day-to-day behavior of ordinary people. Such people are, in any case, sufficiently impressed with their sensory apprehension of individuals and not liable to raise the question of whether or not their thought also reaches directly to the individuality. On the other hand, appreciation of the worth of each individual person seems to be owed not to any epistemology but to the nourishment and enlargement of Greek political philosophy by Christian insight. To this Aquinas' social thought contributed significantly.

merely a subjective postulate but an objective reality, one could not yet conclude that men may hope for an immediate knowledge of God. If such a union were achieved, it would constitute the fullest possible transcendence. Philosophy can go no further than stating as much. At this point Christian belief takes over. Writing now as a theologian, Thomas professes his faith in the gift of a divine elevation to immediate cognitive and affective union with God after death for those who have been loyal in this life. It is this that constitutes perfect happiness.

The theme of immortality that this doctrine raises must, at least, be acknowledged if Thomas' theory of man is not to be truncated. We may begin by recalling that the principle of self-awareness and freedom that is the specific core of the human person is called by Thomas, and by many others, the soul. Aquinas' concern for unifying manifolds of diverse data is demonstrated in his philosophical anthropology, which argues, against many of his contemporaries, that this formal principle of human existence and action is one, not multiple. But it might be asked why it should be supposed that there is any such formal principle at all. That man is corporeal, Thomas would reply, is clear enough. Yet he cannot be merely material since after death the body remains but not life. Nor can the principle of this life be mere corporeality for otherwise every bodily thing would be alive. He concludes to the necessity of a soul, that is to say, to a source of the actuality of the living being, to the principle in virtue of which it lives and acts, as one might say that heat is the principle in virtue of which a glowing iron is hot (*S. Th.*, I, q. 75, a. 1, c.). This example from medieval physics may really be more distracting than helpful. In any case, the notion of a principle of being is hard to grasp since it cannot be imagined, whereas our thinking, as Thomas often pointed out, is always done with the aid of images derived from the sensible world (*S. Th.*, II-II, q. 180, a. 5, ad 2).

In all instances save this one of the human soul, the constitutive principles of a being are never *that which* exists but only principles *by which* the total being exists and operates. The celebrated left tower of Chartres has something that a haphazard pile of an exactly equivalent amount of precisely the same sort of stone has not. This element of beauty and harmony is real, but it does not exist apart from the tower of whose totality it is a constituent. Although this example deals with the accidents of an artificial construction, it may weakly illustrate the Thomistic thesis that maintains that a man's mind is not a thing but a principle by which he thinks. In similar fashion, where his very being is concerned this man is not two things but one flowing from the union of a material and a spiritual principle. Hence, as Thomas observed, we may inexactly speak of the soul understanding or of the eye seeing, but "it is more properly said that a man understands through his soul" (*S. Th.*, I, q. 75, a. 2, ad 2).

As a Christian, Thomas believed in the possibility of man's ultimate resurrection to a new life in a new body whose condition remains mysterious this side of the grave. As a philosopher, he was convinced that one could rationally argue that the human soul, unlike the principle of actuality in plants and beasts, is itself deathless. A summary of this argumentation would impoverish it, so the reader is referred to the established texts in Thomistic philosophy of man.[5] In Aquinas' thought the human spirit is not to be called a pure spirit since its whole function is to be the principle of life in man, who is part animal and part spirit. But the soul is at least partially intellectual, said Thomas, and this points to its immateriality, which, in turn, supposes incorruptibility. Man is mortal but his soul is not. Faith, however, comes in with an assurance beyond philosophy and with the message that man in his wholeness will someday be immortal. St. Thomas summed that up in a passage in his disputation *On Evil*, which Father Gilby has gracefully translated: "Considering the exigencies of the material from which he is made, death and disease are natural to man; but considering his form, immortality is his right, though the principles of nature alone are not sufficient to ensure this: the aptitude is inherent, but the achievement is a gift." [6]

SOME ENDS AND MEANS IN EDUCATION

From Thomas' emphasis upon man as pre-eminently a consciousness-in-the-world there follows quite logically a rather distinctive concept of what education, or specifically human growth, should mean. If one concentrated exclusively on those passages in which Aquinas discusses teaching and learning (*disciplina*) or the dispositions that this process builds up, he might easily conclude that Thomas' educational ideal was pretty much that of Aristotle in the *Ethics* and *Politics*—the highest exercise of the highest power: "Those speculations and thoughts that have their end in themselves and are pursued for their own sake." [7] But such an exclusive concentration would, in fact, lead to serious misapprehension. Thomas' notion of *disciplina* is, as we have remarked, much narrower than our notion of education. It needs to be completed by observing how Thomas, as a Christian theologian, transposes the Aristotelian theme of the "goods of the soul" into a very different key under the inspiration of revelation.

According to the analysis of the *Nicomachean Ethics* the virtuous and truly human life, which constitutes man's highest self-realization and happiness, consists in the occupation of leisure by the full play of reason. In the concrete, this means participation in the distinctive activities of science and the arts, in politics, and, above all, in philosophical contemplation. This requires, to be sure, a sufficiency of material goods and physical well-being as conditions, but the essence of beatitude is to be found in the metaphysical speculations of the virtuous man.

Now Thomas follows this reasoning as far as it goes, but for him it does not go far enough. He will observe that the body does indeed exist to serve the soul just as a tool (*instrumentum*) exists for the sake of the user (*S. Th.*, I, q. 91, a. 3, c.; and II-II, q. 55, a. 1, ad 2). He will further agree that the employment of intelligence is the highest function of man, who is most himself when he is most rational—a point of view subscribed to by many philosophers and scientists. Finally, Thomas agreed with Aristotle that the ultimate goal of all men is happiness, which does consist in a certain sort of knowledge (*S. Th.*, I-II, qq. 1–4). But he would add that the beatifying knowledge that is perfect happiness is not possible in this life—a point of view subscribed to by most ordinary men. Such knowledge, said Thomas, is found only in that direct vision of God that unites the faithful human person to Him after death. But the earthly love and service of God that leads to this fulfillment must be embodied in a practical love of one's fellow men, which requires that we act beneficently toward them all (*S. Th.*, II-II, q. 31, aa. 1–4). For Christianity insists that thought must be completed by action: "He who does the truth comes to the light" (John 3:21). We must be disposed, said Thomas in his commentary on the First Letter to the Corinthians, not merely to understand but also to love and to fulfill in practice that which we know (*In I ad Cor.*, c. II, lect. 1).

The Thomistic philosophical perspective on man also underscores the inadequacy of thinking about education only in terms of intellectual development. For it reminds us that man must be seen as a font of action since to exist is to act: *Agere sequitur esse.* Even a stone continuously repels other objects from pre-empting the space it occupies. But to say that man is intelligent is to say that he is capable of free action, because he can know alternatives that are opposed but not predetermining. At life's countless crossroads we are obliged to decide which of the possible turnings we should reasonably take. The ethical dimension that is the dimension of choice is, therefore, the setting of life and education. This means that the ideal man must be more than a savant, since wisdom does not automatically issue in right decisions inspired by love. An evil man, as Thomas was fond of observing, can be powerfully intelligent, and yet he is not perfectly so (*S. Th.,* II-II, q. 15, a. 3). He lacks prudence, which is precisely the intellectual disposition to direct one's life rationally and therefore morally.

When the Thomistic educational ideal has been completed by these ethical and theological considerations, it is easy to see that it differs from the excessively academic goal of leisure devoted to contemplation. Nevertheless, in line with the traditional doctrine that the gift of divine love called "grace" perfects human nature without suppressing it, Thomas would have held that Christianity does not aim to supplant an authentic humanism but rather to enfold and transform it. Growth in the capacity for true intellectualism remains, therefore, an important part of the educational objective that his thought implies and this is worth saying something more about.

GROWTH IN WISDOM

An educator who accepted Thomas' idea of man would appropriately draw conclusions from each of the emphases in that concept. Because man is partially spiritual, the growth of intelligence is a central phase of his fulfillment. But because man is not a pure spirit, this development necessarily takes place in time and through a processive interaction with the world he experiences. For man, in Aquinas' thought, is that unique kind of conscious being whose spirit requires by its very nature to be embodied and to have an historical existence if it is to know and so to love and to choose. This singular existential condition has results directly related to the fact that man is both partially spiritual and partially material. The significance of the interplay of these two principles for the psychic life is indicated when Thomas refers to some of the requisites for learning.

The first of these conditions is sense experience, which is needed if we are to think at all. In the *Commentary on the Sentences* Aquinas remarks that we know other things exist either because we sense them (and this requires having a body) or because we can at least reason to their existence from some sensory data. Thus we conclude to the fact of a fire from the sight of smoke (Bk. III, d. 23, q. 1, a. 2). It is particularly through our eyes, ears, and touch, he thinks, that we are immediately conjoined with reality. He illustrated this obvious point with the examples of a blind man's ignorance of color and of the inhibition of reason in those who are asleep or delirious (S. Th., I, q. 101, a. 2, c.). Indeed, he once described experience itself as the knowing of individual objects through the senses (S. Th., I, q. 54, a. 5, c.). Although one could reasonably take experience in a wider way than that, still the importance for learning of this sensory contact with the world, which is our natural soil and climate, seems as plain as our need for air.

Yet in St. Thomas' lifetime the schools did not much honor this fact. Elementary education meant memorizing a book, and university education meant listening. When in the seventeenth century Comenius called for systematically encouraging children to look at and listen to all that lay about them, this was novel enough to be labeled "Sense Realism" in subsequent histories of education. It may well be, of course, that thirteenth-century parents also invited their children to notice and name the inhabitants and furniture of the household and barnyard. It would have been, in any case, the beginning of wisdom for those children, since, as Thomas once said, man is not an angel, and the proper objects of his mind "are the natures of material things . . . apprehended through sense and imagination" (S. Th., I, q. 84, a. 7, c.). This theme of the indispensability of sense experience is, in fact, so central in Thomistic learning-theory that one study argues that for Aquinas the general notion of learning is the acquisition and organization of images, while specifically intellectual learnings ideally terminate in judgments about the reality of our experience.[8]

The distinctive effects of man's psychosomatic unity are also adverted to whenever Thomas notices how bodily structures and dispositions, which he sometimes called the *complexio corporis,* affect both learning and temperament. Those with the finest bodies, he thought, have the more powerful minds (S. Th., I, q. 85, a. 7, c.). Aristotle had convinced him that the kinesthetic sense is the foundation of all the others and that its acuteness depends upon the balance maintained among the elements of the body. So he more than once lays it down that those who have more perfect bodies have a more refined sense of touch and, consequently, keener intelligence (S. Th., I, q. 76, a. 5, c.; q. 91, a. 1, ad 3; q. 101, a. 2, c.). It was, no doubt, his own informal observation that taught him how pain and strong emotion can block learning. In addition, he had a theory that bodily dispositions may not only incline a person to be robust or sickly but may temperamentally predispose him toward certain character traits, so that he is naturally apt to be meek rather than fiery, chaste rather than otherwise (S. Th., I-II, q. 51, a. 1, c.).

Nor are these somatic states the only conditioners of thinking. Our affective dispositions are also influential. This insight emerges from an analysis of the dynamism of any free human action. Love, in a certain root sense, is the source of all such uncoerced activity. For whoever acts, says Thomas, acts for the sake of a good that he finds in some sense lovable. All love implies the recognizing and seeking of a value even if it be only the benefit of sidestepping an evil (*S. Th.*, I-II, q. 28, a. 6, c.). Thomas agrees with Aristotle and Dewey that we do best the things we like to do (*S. Th.*, II-II, q. 15, a. 3, c.). That is to say, a student is most effectively motivated when the learning task is seen by him as intrinsically worthwhile.

A few years before his death in World War I, Pierre Rousselot, a creative Thomistic thinker, published a perceptive essay which argued that profound affective dispositions actually heighten perception itself.[9] The optimist, for instance, penetrates to the encouraging or smiling aspects of any situation, while the pessimist can say of them all, with Jaques in *As You Like It*: "I can suck melancholy out of a song as a weasel sucks eggs." Love, far from being blind, really empowers the lover to perceive qualities hidden from the indifferent. Every great teacher appreciates this insight whether or not he has formulated it consciously. He knows, as Thomas did, that man's natural interest in learning is all too easily paralyzed when it collides with barriers set up by lack of talent, by cares, anxieties, and laziness (*CG*, b. I, c. 4). A sufficiently strong response to intellectual values will enable the learner to vault these hurdles, and the great teacher is the one who knows how to awaken such a response. For what is willed out of love, Thomas commented, is willed more intensely than what is willed out of fear (*CG*, b. III, c. 116).

Aquinas frequently made the point that moral behavior also influences the life of thought. This is, after all, only a particular case of that wider interplay between man's volitional and mental activity that he once summarized by remarking that the mind and the will are mutually inclusive (S. Th., I, q. 16, a. 4, ad 1). Indeed, the very notion of morality implies this reciprocity since it signifies the rational ordering of conduct (S. Th., II-II, q. 47, a. 7, c.; and q. 168, a. 1, c.). Conversely, Thomas describes evil as a falling away from right reason into the slavery of beasts. The theologian, however, will see in such failures the formality of sin or offense against God, while the philosopher regards them primarily as irrationalities (S. Th., II-II, q. 64, a. 2, ad 3; I-II, q. 71, a. 6, ad 5). But so far as learning is concerned, the practical conclusion is the same in either case. Aquinas observes, therefore, that both the child and the intemperate adult find learning hard because they are both torn away from reasonableness by sensual appetites (S. Th., II-II, q. 142, a. 2, c.). But, as he adds in his commentary on Aristotle's Physics, if young people develop strong moral character, they may overcome these impediments. A good life predisposes men to think soundly since it damps down "the vehemence of the passions and the tumult raised by external businesses" (S. Th., II-II, q. 180, a. 2, c.). It is not that carnal vices, for instance, directly alter intelligence, but rather that they hobble it by tying it down to images of food or sex. So, too, the man possessed by grief, anger, jealousy, or pride reasons that much less effectively. Immoral people do, of course, perform brilliantly upon occasion but not as consistently or as well as they might (S. Th., II-II, q. 15, a. 3). In one Summa passage Thomas applies this to his own discipline. Knowledge, he writes, is both speculative and affective. However learned, therefore, the proud theologian may be, he will lack that precious affective insight that soars beyond mere erudition. For self-love has displaced in him the love of truth (S. Th., II-II, q. 162, a. 3, ad 1).

It is worthwhile to winnow the great mass of the *Summa* for these brief allusions because they prove that Thomas knew well enough that man is not a completely intellectual being. He did not, it is true, elaborate this point with any wealth of theory or empirical detail. The comments we have gathered together here are mostly un-exceptional. But the genius of the Thomistic synthesis shows itself in the way it allows for logically inserting later findings. Freud's inquiries have abundantly enlarged Thomas' remark that the human soul is only partially intellective and these contributions can be harmoniously integrated with the concept of man as a "spirit-in-the-world."

One of those contributions is a keener realization of the truth that we are beings with a history. Not so much that we are shaped by living in one or other epoch, al-though this is true enough, as that we are irrevocably fashioned by our life's own local story. As a psychologist colleague of the writer once put it: "If you are born in the Bronx, you never get over it completely." To be hu-man is to be historical because one lives at this time, not that; in this community and not elsewhere. Education must, therefore, take into account the influence of this social and historical setting, for its impact is ineluctable whether recognized or not.

Aquinas did acknowledge that social dimension, al-though he did not emphasize it as we should today. In his moral philosophy he observes that man is naturally a social animal only able to mature within the family and civic communities.[10] And just because men are social an-imals, they must develop formal speech and writing for they cannot live together unless they share one another's thoughts (*In lib. Peri Her.*, b. I, lect. 2). This suggests some consideration of what Thomas had to say about teaching. For a man's need to be helped by others within a community is nicely exemplified in his need for some teaching, while the teacher, in his turn, finds language to be his best tool.

ON TEACHING

To take learning in its widest connotation serves very usefully to emphasize the truth that we must learn our way through life. The infant needs to learn how to respond to a smile, and the old man needs to learn acceptance of age's deteriorations. But we have already noted that *disciplina* is only used by Thomas for one sort of intellectual learning. His theory of *habitus,* however, which is the context for his reflections on this learning product, is applicable to many types of learning: the strictly scientific; the development of skills in the arts or growth in character. *Habitus* is the technical Latin term for Aristotle's *hexis* and is best rendered, as a recent translator points out, by "disposition." [11] The concept is verified in all those cases in which a capacity for action can be developed so that one is constituted midway between actuality and the sheer potentiality of those who possess no such disposition. Thus the man who knows calculus or can paint a picture has the disposition of science or art. It is a true entitative enlargement of his person whether he is actually employing it or not. The courageous man is, to that extent, more fully human than the coward since he has a real ability to confront dangers steadfastly. When a plumber has mastered his craft, his capacity for rational and manual action has been heightened, and he exists more fully than he previously did. These dispositions strengthening a man's capacity for thought or for practical action or for ethical consistency were called by Thomas intellectual or moral virtues.

He believed that such virtues were built up by steady effort and that this process could, in the case of some intellectual dispositions, be expedited by a teacher. This becomes possible, as we noted above, when there is a question of acquiring skills in deductive scientific thinking. It is in this context that Thomas talked about teaching, and he used Euclidean geometry as the archetype of the sciences that could be taught. Nevertheless, his reflections on the teacher's art have a wider application than that.

What is striking about these reflections is the modest importance Thomas attached to the teacher's work. There are, he says, two ways of learning. The better is the way of independent investigation, which he calls "discovery" (*inventio*). It is remarkably illustrated in the exploits of gifted children who teach themselves to read or, like the three-year-old Mozart, to play a musical instrument before having had any instruction. We all employ this method in less spectacular fashion when we acquire some store of knowledge or some skill through our own experience and effort. This procedure not only manifests greater intellectual power in the learner, Thomas thought, but is also more perfect. For we learn in this case through an immediate contact with the realities in question, whereas, when we are taught, the teacher's signs (generally verbal ones) intervene and, at best, point us toward those realities (*De Ver.*, q. 11, an. 1 and 2, ad 4; *S. Th.*, I, q. 117, n. 1; and III, q. 12, a. 3, ad 2). It is a rare talent, nonetheless, that can wholly dispense with a teacher's help and to do so is, in any case, time consuming. So that the chief value of this second way of learning, that is to say, learning-through-teaching (*disciplina*), is one of economy. Most men would have neither the leisure nor the courage to learn all they need to know if teachers did not ease and accelerate the process for them.

Thomas' basic recommendation for teachers actually underlines the primacy of that personal way of discovery. For the teacher, he says, should pattern his method after the one naturally used when a man learns by himself. This is based on a more general principle which holds

that whenever an effect can be produced either by nature or by art, the method of art should be the same as
that of nature. Since teaching is an art, we must expect
to find it most effective when its procedures are most like
those of independent search. Far from urging a sharp
dichotomy between learning-by-discovery and learning-
by-instruction, Thomas suggested that wise teaching nar-
rows the difference between them. A good teacher con-
trives for his students an experience as much like that of
learning-by-discovery as possible.

Thomas illustrates this point from an analogous situation and thereby significantly illuminates his own concept of the teacher's role. The example is that of a physician ministering to a man brought down by an infection.
In many such cases, if the patient went unattended, his
body would mobilize its restorative forces and eventually
heal itself. The physician's medications operate by re-
enforcing those natural bodily functions and hastening
the cure. The art of the teacher is like that of this intern-
ist, since all the teacher can hope to do is to strengthen
the student's resources and facilitate their exercise (*De
Ver.*, q. 11, a. 1, c.). The import of the analogy is clear
enough whether it is medically accurate or not. Whenever true learning occurs, its principal cause is the learner
himself. In Thomas' terminology the teacher is called a
secondary and instrumental cause—helpful but not indispensable. He cannot transfer his own knowledge to
the student but only help him achieve similar learning
for himself.

The sciences that formally verify this concept of
teaching employ syllogistic reasoning from evident premises for the accumulation of an ordered body of demonstrated knowledge. The premises may be self-evident
or derived from experimentation or from another and
higher science. It is the teacher's job to provide the student with some insight either into these basic principles
or into the process of unfolding their implications. But

since all thinking begins with sense awareness, the teacher must exploit some sensory experiences that will help the learner arrive at appropriate concepts and judgments. This procedure might be reduced to a simple pointing. If a man were baffled by a wall too high to leap, the teacher could turn him about so that he might see the ladder leaning against the shed behind him. At a more sophisticated level, teaching uses signs that are artificial pointers defined by Thomas as sensible objects leading to knowledge of things not yet known (*S. Th.*, I, q. 117, a. 1, ad 3; *De Ver.*, q. 11, a. 1, ad 11). Of all such surrogates for immediate experience, the most common and resourceful is the word.

For the teacher's words are sensed, by the eye or ear, and they are signs pointing beyond themselves. Indeed, unless the learner does get beyond them to the reality they signify, his learning is only a mean sort of verbalism. But the teacher's art consists precisely in employing language so skillfully that this transit is actually made. It is fair to say that for Thomas the great teacher is a great rhetorician in the radical sense: a man who can adapt words to his purpose in the most telling manner. If he has this power over language, he can communicate his own thinking in a useful way because he can select the words that will function effectively as signs. He will command a wealth of metaphor and example all designed to stimulate and guide the student to engender in himself the desired intellectual dispositions.[12]

For when teaching succeeds, the learners have experienced a true growth. The *habitus* of science, as Thomas might say, has been born within them. They did not begin with innate ideas, but they did have an innate capacity and desire for knowledge and a grasp of such fundamental laws of thought as the one that declares the incompatibility of simultaneous affirmation and negation of one and the same proposition (*CG*, b. II, c. 83). A common language serves as the bridge between the teacher and these learners. Thus the stage is set for the generation of knowledge, as Thomas called it in his commentary on Aristotle's *Posterior Analytics*:

> *Generation is the reduction from potency to act. What is learned, then, was not fully known beforehand, as Plato maintained, nor fully unknown. . . . But it was known potentially or virtually in the knowledge of universal principles. As knowledge in the strict sense, it was actually unknown. And so to learn means to be brought from the condition of potential, virtual, or general knowledge to actual knowledge in the proper sense* [In lib. Post. Anal., *b. I, lect.* 3].

We may wonder, perhaps, how Thomas would have specified this global statement. What subjects would he have included in a curriculum and in what order? There is a passage in his commentary on Boethius' tract on the Trinity which touches upon this question, but it only amounts to a ratification of the traditional seven liberal arts as the best preparation for the master's program in philosophy (*Expositio super librum Boethii De Trinitate,* q. 5, a. 1, ad 3). In theory this was not a bad scheme, for the *trivium* of language disciplines and the *quadrivium* of mathematical disciplines constituted a reconciliation in one curriculum of those "two cultures," which C. P. Snow believes to have been so unhappily divorced in the twentieth century. But in Thomas' day the Parisian arts course had actually developed beyond this older program. Logic and the Aristotelian philosophy and science were then ascendant.

In his commentary on the Sixth Book of the *Nichomachean Ethics,* Thomas has some remarks about curriculum that are more characteristic of his own outlook than the passage in the *De Trinitate.* They are rooted in his convictions about the importance of sense knowledge, direct experience, and moral rectitude if one wants to advance in learning. They also, of course, echo Aristotle, since Thomas is expounding the philosopher's opinion that boys can learn mathematics but don't have enough experience to become physicists or philosophers. Thomas concludes, therefore, that a suitable curriculum would begin with the study of logic or method of inquiry. Then the students would move on to mathematics, which doesn't demand maturity and does allow for the use of such sense images as those of numerals and figures. After mathematics, boys are ready for natural philosophy (physics), which requires rather more extensive experience but still does not leave the realm of sensation entirely behind. This is to be followed by moral philosophy, which calls for considerable knowledge of the human condition, since this is the source from which it derives its premises. It also needs some solidity of character so that one's thinking will not be colored by passion. Last of all come the studies of wisdom and divinity (metaphysics and theology), for which one must have a strong intelligence that can transcend the sphere of sense and imagination (*In lib. Eth.*, b. VI, lect. 7).

Contemporary educators will naturally find too restrictive this limiting of the concepts of teaching and learning to the special instances of the deductive sciences or those which have both an inductive and deductive moment. Do we not need to know how the arts are taught, including the art of practical thinking? We do indeed, but we shall not find this account in Thomas' writings. We shall find, however, the place at which to incorporate the insight of those pedagogical pioneers who developed the techniques of "learning by doing."

It will be recalled that Thomas followed Aristotle in distinguishing two prime sorts of intellectual activities: those ordered to understanding the world and those ordered to changing it. Consequently, when he philosophizes about intellectual excellence, he distinguishes the dispositions that perfect speculative thinking from those which do the same for practical thought. In the first group he puts the ability to grasp basic premises ("understanding"), the various sorts of scientific learning ("science"), and the architectonic power of perceiving relationships linking disparate realities and particular truths. This last is called "Wisdom," and Thomas regards it as man's highest natural intellectual excellence. For he who is wise understands how all things are related to each other and to God from whom they come and to whom they go.

But beside these speculative "virtues" there are other enlargements of intelligence that enhance creative power. These are the arts, which Thomas defines as fundamentally "the right way of making things" (S. Th., I-II, q. 57, a. 3, c.). This definition frees the notion of art from limitation to the so-called fine arts or to the museum and introduces the aesthetic element into the stuff of ordinary life. There is a right way to drive a car or bake a cake, just as there is a right way to design a bridge, paint a picture, or write a lyric. In every case, the successful product is no lucky fluke but the issue of an intelligence powerfully controlling its materials. An art is an abiding disposition, for the good cook and the good poet perform consistently.

They could have acquired such excellence, however, in only one way—by practice. Of course, the excellencies of speculative intelligence are also generated by appropriate and, usually, repeated action. The would-be geometer must do a lot of problems before he really understands how the Euclidean propositions devolve from the theorems. But in the development of artistic skills the practice naturally consists in overt action—in doing the art. Surely the same is true for the development of practical, problem-solving ability. Thomas' portrait of the prudent man implies as much. For the prudent man is skilled in judging wisely and well as to how he should behave, and he reaches this enviable condition by practice. But that is not all. He must also acquire those moral dispositions that guarantee that he will conform his behavior to his sound prudential judgments with at least reasonable regularity. This reminds us not to overlook the ethical dimension if we would make any adequate distillation of the themes in Thomism that have educational relevance.

THE GOOD MAN

Since Aquinas did not intend to write a philosophy of education as we would understand it, he does not advert to character development when talking about the teacher (*magister*) or learning (*disciplina*). This doesn't mean, however, that he simply equated human excellence with knowledge and intellectual power. It is clear, if his work is taken as a whole, that he presumes a complete man will both know and live the truth but didn't think the second inevitably follows upon the first even though it presupposes it. The desirable dispositions that enhance intelligence may be called "virtues" (*virtus*, i.e., "strength"), he wrote in the *Summa*, because they strengthen the mind in its good functioning, which is the considering of truth. But they are not virtues in the sense of insuring the morally good use of this capacity. For a scientist to employ his powers well it is necessary that he have such moral dispositions as justice and love (*S. Th.*, I-II, q. 57, a. 1, c.).

This accent upon moral virtue would hardly startle the great educational theorists, for many of them have been even more emphatic, although they may differ among themselves about the precise nature of morality. Plato's philosophy of education is set within his wider concern for defining the truly good life. Quintilian said that only a good man can be truly eloquent and that, if one cannot be both, it is better to be virtuous than to be fluent. Rousseau aimed to bring Emile up in such wise as to keep "his heart from vice and the spirit of error." For Dewey the problems of conduct are life's central issues, and he argues in *Moral Principles in Education* that a teacher's chief business is to see that the greatest possible number of ideas acquired by young people are so acquired as to become true motive forces of conduct. St. Thomas is well within this tradition when, in the *Summa contra Gentiles,* he ranks values hierarchically in terms of their relationship to man's ultimate goal of perfect happiness and assigns first place to moral virtue because it nourishes the good life that leads to that beatitude. Intellectual excellence is put second.

This kind of talk makes some people restive. Scholars are apt to find Thomas' intellectualism agreeable enough even if they are not much taken with its metaphysical rationale. But quarrels are liable to be provoked when the question of moral values is introduced because the theoretical contexts are diverse even in the case of such widely appreciated dispositions as honesty, friendliness, and responsibility in the exercise of freedom. St. Thomas' moral ideal, for instance, cannot be fully inscribed within the circle of philosophy. For just as his religious belief led him to transform the Aristotelian ideal of wisdom, so as a Christian he has a theological understanding of the history and character of man as a moral agent.

It is neither possible nor necessary to summarize that theology here, but its outlines may be briefly recalled. According to the Christian vision of history, man was destined for a beatifying fulfillment in a life of immediate union with God. Since this would transcend anything of which he could naturally conceive or be capable, it must be a wholly gratuitous gift of infinite and divine love. Sin, however, meant the loss of this opportunity and the alienation of man until the salvific life and death of Jesus, the Lord, overcame that estrangement and founded a new "People of God." History is, therefore, the perilous and glorious ascending of the human race to its divinely appointed fulfillment. This depends finally upon God, who, says Thomas, is always working to make men holy as the sun is always lighting up the air (*S. Th.*, II-II, q. 4, a. 4, ad 3). But since men are free they can compromise or oppose this work. If a man's life embodies a love of God and a congruous love of his fellow-men, it is good and advances him toward the joyful vision. It is worth noting that this morality dynamized by the desire for perfect happiness is not a refined hedonism. For it denies that beatitude is to be found in any of the goods that might be sought on the pleasure principle: wealth, honor, fame, power, health, or delight itself (*S. Th.*, I-II, q. 2). The happiness that is called heaven consists rather in that incomprehensible and overflowing intuition in which God is loved for Himself. Nevertheless, Thomas adds, joy companions this union even as heat accompanies fire (*S. Th.*, I-II, q. 4, a. 1, c.).

In building up his moral philosophy, then, Aquinas draws upon both his philosophical and his religious convictions. Some of the byways he explores seem quaint today when we are not given to weighing the liceity of cosmetics. But much of this ethic's substance formulates the perennial moral persuasions of civilized peoples. The "natural law" proscribing murder or dishonesty is only, as Aquinas remarked on occasion, man's native intelligence judging which values should be sought and which evils avoided. Since this "law" is born within us, no one is basically ignorant of it. We all know, said Thomas, that we should treat others as we would wish to be treated ourselves (*In duo Praecepta Caritatis*, a. 1). The application of these broad principles to concrete situations is, to be sure, more difficult and uncertain. In the Commentary on the *Ethics* Thomas says that the individual concerned must be the judge of the case in light of its circumstances. But the moralist can offer some help by indicating the solution that usually holds in such questions (*In lib. Eth.*, b. II, lect. 2). Christianity, however, may transpose the issue to quite another plane and teach men to love others not merely as they love themselves, but as Christ has loved them. One would not see Thomas' moral teaching in the round, if this dimension of revelation were omitted.

Two master themes in that teaching must be pointed out as this chapter is concluded, for they have considerable resonance for education. After all, in education we are always choosing from among alternative ends and means, and the realm of choice is the realm of morality. The first theme is that of *freedom*, which is the presupposition of a truly human and good life, and the second is *friendship*, in which such a life finds its fulfillment. These are keystones in any Christian moral theory and hence in Thomism. The theory observes that, while men may sometimes act unconsciously or under constraint, it is only when they are acting voluntarily that they behave in fully personal fashion. This is particularly the case when rational self-possession is mature enough for a free and deliberate choice. It cannot be said that Thomas worked out all the concrete implications of freedom or analyzed its structure as searchingly as contemporary existentialists and phenomenologists have done. But the theme could hardly be more central to his concept of the person who is pictured as necessarily capable of freedom just because he is intelligent. Indeed, a philosophy of education inspired by Thomism might logically organize itself around the notion and the nourishment of freedom and of wisdom.

The idea of freedom, however, easily directs our attention beyond itself to the values toward which it tends. Now, said St. Thomas, love is the name we give to the dynamism drawing us toward the goals we seek. You might even speak of a stone falling toward earth from a certain connatural love for its center (*S. Th.*, I-II, q. 26, a. 1, c.). But we know love best from our own experience, which shows it to be twofold. The love for some things is chiefly a desire to possess them and the joy they bring. So, Aquinas remarked, we may be said to love wine or a horse, but it would be ridiculous to speak of making friends of these things (*S. Th.*, II-II, q. 23, a. 1, c.). The love that really deserves the name of friendship is compounded of benevolence and affection. It involves both mutual communication and a wishing-well to the other, who is cherished for himself and not as an object assuaging desire. This love of friendship finds its noblest expression in the disposition called *caritas,* which is so opaquely translated "charity." *Caritas* is the friendship with God that lifts a man higher in this life than his thought can ever do. For when a man loves God, he is directly united to Him, since love always joins the lover to the beloved (*S. Th.*, I-II, q. 28, a. 1, ad 3; and I, q. 108, a. 6, ad 3).

Union is, indeed, love's distinctive effect wherever love is found, and so friendship is the source of human community. As it varies in intensity, so does the perfection of the communion. The strongest possible human friendship, wrote Thomas, is that between a man and his wife, where the union is not only physical but extends to a total and permanent sharing of family life (*CG*, b. III, c. 123). When the two minds are also indivisibly conjoined, the marriage is perfect (*S. Th.*, III, q. 29, a. 2). But we are also acquainted with less intimate societies of friendship. Indeed, Thomas thought that we could not be happy on earth without friends whom we may love and by whom we are sustained (*S. Th.*, I-II, q. 4, a. 8, c.). Finally, friendship does an indispensable work when it accounts for our living together as a commonwealth rather than as a herd.

In St. Thomas' philosophy the political community is not simply a useful convention but the expression of human nature's social dimension. But this community would never have risen above the level of a mob or a flock unless

there had been among its members some surrender of ego-
ism and some concern for the welfare of others. A tyrant
might, indeed, promote the state as a way of promoting
himself, but this is not what good citizenship means (*De
Caritate*, a. 2). It is true that human persons are the most
perfect thing in nature and cannot, therefore, be wholly
subordinated even to the needs of their own community.
Yet it is natural for a good man to risk his life for the republic since it is natural for him to be, in a sense, part of
a whole greater than himself (*S. Th.*, I, q. 60, a. 5, c.).
In fact, the theme of friendship unifies the manifold of
value itself. For the perfection of life consists supremely
in friendship with God, which, in turn, embodies and
proves itself in the friendship that creates the human
community without which the person could not exist.
Thus the individual and the social aims of education are
themselves harmonized and unified.

❖ NOTES ❖

1. See the remarks of Manning M. Patillo, Jr., and Donald
   M. Mackenzie, *Church-Sponsored Higher Education in
   the United States: Report of the Danforth Commission*
   (Washington, D.C.: American Council on Education,
   1966), pp. 12–13.
2. See the appendix on "Scientific Knowledge" by Anthony
   Kenny in his translation of the *Summa Theologiae*, I-II,
   qq. 49–54: *St. Thomas Aquinas: Summa Theologiae*,
   Vol. 22: *Dispositions for Human Acts* (New York: Mc-
   Graw-Hill, 1964), p. 134.
3. Many of these short comments can be uncovered by consulting the *Tabula Aurea*, a general index to Thomas'
   works, under such headings as *addiscere, discere, docere,
   puer, scientia, signum, studere, studium, veritas,* and
   their cognates. This index was published by the Domini-

can Peter of Bergamo in 1473. A photo-offset from the Vivès edition of 1880 was issued in 1960: Peter of Bergamo, *In Opera Sancti Thomae Aquinatis Index seu Tabula Aurea* (Rome: Editiones Paulinae, 1960).

4. Paul Lafargue, "Reminiscences of Marx," in C. P. Dutt, ed., *Karl Marx, Selected Works* (New York: International Publishers, 1936), Vol. I, p. 87. These reminiscences first appeared in 1890.

5. See, for instance, J. F. Donceel, S.J., *Philosophical Psychology*, 2nd ed. rev. (New York: Sheed and Ward, 1961), pp. 330–339; and George P. Klubertanz, S.J., *The Philosophy of Human Nature* (New York: Appleton-Century-Crofts, 1953), pp. 312–316.

6. *De Malo*, q. 5, a. 5, *St. Thomas Aquinas: Philosophical Texts*, trans. Thomas Gilby (London: Oxford University Press, 1951), p. 174.

7. Aristotle, *Politics*, trans. H. Rackham (Cambridge: Harvard University Press, 1959), vii 3, 1325b 20, p. 551.

8. Tad W. Guzie, S.J., *The Analogy of Learning: An Essay Toward a Thomistic Psychology of Learning* (New York: Sheed and Ward, 1960). See particularly pp. 185, 187.

9. Pierre Rousselot, "Amour spirituel et synthèse aperceptive," *Revue de Philosophie*, XVI (March, 1910), 225–240.

10. On this point see Gilby, *op. cit.*, pp. 367–393, as well as Father Gilby's own study, *Between Community and Society: A Philosophy and Theology of the State* (New York: Longmans, Green, 1953).

11. Kenny, *op. cit.*, p. xxi. See also Vernon J. Bourke, "The Role of Habitus in the Thomistic Metaphysics of Potency and Act," in R. E. Brennan, O.P., ed., *Essays in Thomism* (New York: Sheed and Ward, 1942), pp. 103–109.

12. For a twentieth-century echo of this theme see William Walsh, *The Use of Imagination* (London: Chatto and Windus, 1959), p. 229: "The quality of an education depends most on the quality of the teacher and the qual-

ity of the teacher is best indicated by his use of language." In S. *Th.*, q. 111, a. 4, c., Thomas observes that, in addition to knowledge of the premises and conclusions of his science, a teacher must possess an "abundance of examples."

Afterword:
On the Relevance
of Thomism for
Education Today

A *woman who has written* distinguished studies of religious questions has said:

> Whenever I poke my nose into a volume of the Summa, both the approach to the problems and the problems themselves strike me as utterly remote and abstruse: nothing for me, it just doesn't apply; it's all as uninteresting as it is incomprehensible. I feel myself rebelling inwardly, as though I were forcing myself to read a book about income tax. It's a foreign language. The door is open, but I don't want to go in.[1]

This sort of chilly reaction, as was noted earlier, is common enough. Even at its height the interest in Thomism was largely confined to Catholic academic circles, and now it has sharply declined from the peak it reached there during the first half of this century. Since intellectual styles have a cyclic rhythm, it would be incautious to conclude that Thomism will never again be so popular, but at the moment it surely is not. Some decades ago secular critics judged it too theological; today young Catholic thinkers reject it as excessively intellectualistic. Yet it would be unenlightening to attribute Thomism's change in fortunes to limitations in Aquinas' thought, for there are limitations in every philosopher's thought. It is rather that the gaps in Thomism are the sort that trouble men of today and put them off, while its strengths are not of the sort that attract them. When Thomas philosophized, he asked certain questions that twentieth-century philosophers judge of little importance, and he omitted others that they consider most pertinent. Of course, the inadequacy of his interest in history is no more conspicuous than, let us say, Marx's disinterest in religion. But it is more unfashionable. Moreover, when Thomas did handle questions that have remained insistent, his methodology and, often enough, his solutions differed from those common nowadays. So criticisms of Thomism indict aspects both of its procedure and of its content as the disenchantment of Ida Görres quoted above indicates.

Thomism is found uncongenial, for instance, because of its systematic character. For although the general notion of a system is respectable enough in science and engineering, most contemporary philosophers think of it as a marsh light. Thomas, however, went about ordering a vast library of topics into an organic whole through the instrumentality of basic principles and nuclear concepts. Not only has he an orchestrated vision of God, man, and the universe, but he works it down into precise answers to a multitude of specific questions. This wide-ranging confidence makes a bad impression. "Unrealistic and illusory" are the adjectives applied to the system precisely as such by an American Dominican.[2]

Yet we might employ here an instructive distinction that Dorothy Sayers formulated while reflecting on different sorts of poetry. Then we will say that St. Thomas wrote a philosophy of statement rather than a philosophy of search. The former would be chiefly interested in arriving at conclusions; the latter, in displaying the complexity of the problem and the variety of paths leading toward tentative solutions. Both kinds of philosophy are good, as Miss Sayers said of the two types of poetry.[3] But they appeal to different ages. In the thirteenth century, when Western civilization was freeing itself from the crudities of life and thought that marked it a few hundred years earlier, Thomas' powerful assertion of rationality may have been just the sort of bracing corroboration needed, whether the attitude was original with him or only the voicing of a widely felt conviction. His whole intellectual endeavor, in any case, amounted to a balanced affirmation of the possibilities of reason for the introduction of order into the turbulence of human experience. He once observed in the *Summa* that human institutions need to be changed, if they can be improved. In philosophy itself there is progress as the theories of early thinkers are perfected.

> *The same holds true in practical affairs. The first men who tried to devise something useful for the human community created imperfect institutions with many defects because they were unable to take all factors into consideration. Their successors introduced changes and institutions which less often fell short of serving the general utility* (S. Th., I-II, q. 97, a. 1, c.).

Most men would not struggle to make life more humane and rational, if they did not have a similar trust in the likelihood of some success. But despite the scientific and technological triumphs of rationality, or perhaps on that very account, people are now less sure about the basic intelligibility of the universe than medieval men appear to have been. Either we know it to be less fixed than they supposed and man himself to be less reasonable, or at least we pay more attention to process and the unconscious and prefer an illuminating dissection of the issue to a clear but abstract explanation.

This systematic character of Thomism is not its only controversial feature. Aquinas' method also disconcerts many people and particularly those who do not share his religious faith. For he weaves his philosophizing in and out of a theological texture. The *Summa* begins with the question of God, which surely remains a lively topic but scarcely constitutes modern philosophy's take-off point. Because Thomas' philosophical essays are scattered about in his theological discourse, they are rather inaccessible to begin with, and besides that their experiential origins are not spelled out in great detail. Justice Holmes once observed that philosophizing is "the chief end of man— but it is only useful when expended on a copious supply of crude facts." [4] Thomas would have agreed. "To theorize about universal ideas without previous induction is not possible," he noted in his commentary on the first book of the *Posterior Analytics*.[5] But he doesn't take his readers through that induction, step by step from its start in a close inventory of the experiential data. A final methodological obstacle is thrown up by his terminology, which is heavily Aristotelian and goes pretty much unexplained.[6] This is particularly confusing when Thomas gives those terms a special meaning of his own. That encourages the phenomenon of commentators centuries after his death arriving for the first time at an appreciation of what he meant by *esse* or of how this notion of existence is the key to his metaphysics.

Besides its procedures, the substance of Thomism

also disappoints many students today, partly because
problems are developed with little reference either to the
historical context in which they pose themselves and the
philosopher thinks of them or to the conditions of the
subject, that philosopher who does the thinking. Some
contemporary studies have shown that Thomism is not
incompatible with these perspectives.[7] But Thomas himself did not probe either the interior life or the concrete
historical process. Of course, he has strengths of another
sort, and a book like M. Gilson's *The Christian Philosophy of St. Thomas Aquinas* makes these impressively
clear. The ordinary reader, in fact, is likely to find Thomism more acceptable than do professional philosophers.
For the great themes of Aquinas' theistic realism are profound refinements of what might still be called a com-
monsense tradition in epistemology and ethics, even
though it does not prevail in current technical studies.
No doubt there are fashions in philosophy as there are
in the arts. But one does not think less of Mozart because
twentieth-century musicians write in a different idiom or
of Velasquez because abstractions are now popular. The
larger public, indeed, prefers Mozart to Schoenberg, and
Hopper and Wyeth to abstract expressionism. So there
may be some point to the remark of the Anglican theologian, J. V. Langmead Casserley, who has said that
most people are ready for Thomas' arguments for the
existence of God.[9]

Here, though, we are chiefly interested in asking
whether any of Thomas' intellectual attitudes are nor-
mative for contemporary educational theory and practice.
It is fair to say that he did not himself influence school
procedures or contribute to their theory. He had no significant involvement with the structures either of the
school or of the larger society as a Horace Mann or a
Karl Marx did. Nor did he tackle the issues that have
engrossed those thinkers who did shape education in the
Atlantic community. This is not surprising. We should

hardly have expected a developed concern for child-nature or adolescent psychology from one who was in a Benedictine monastery at five during a century when teen-agers were generals and kings. But we do feel the absence of this sort of interest when Thomas discusses the role of the teacher. He was himself a remarkably dedicated and kindly master, but the conception set out in the *De Magistro* is surely too impersonal.[9] Inevitably so, of course, since it is cast in the highly technical form of the medieval *quaestio,* which dictated this sort of treatment. But a complete philosophy of teaching must go on to point out that teachers may choose to treat their students either as objects or as fellow persons but can hardly avoid doing one or the other and taking the consequences. It is true that some theoreticians of the teaching machine have envisioned an even more detached pedagogy and unblinkingly look forward to the day when each school child is isolated in a soundproof cubicle with electronic wizards to instruct him. But this concept of learning is closer to Thomas' analysis of the generation of scientific knowledge than it is to Dewey's emphasis upon the school as a society or to Buber's insight into the importance of a personal encounter between teacher and pupil. Thomas, in fact, would probably have preferred the human teacher to the machine even for strictly deductive learnings, because the former can adapt language and procedure more flexibly than any machines to date can.

It will be more profitable by way of conclusion, however, to indicate some characteristics of Aquinas' mind and work that remain instructive. Their selection is quite arbitrary, of course, but perhaps we may list six themes that are still relevant for school practice because they are not confined either to the speculative context of Thomism or to the historical context of the thirteenth century, although we may conceptualize them differently than Thomas did.

The first of these is Aquinas' affirmation of the dignity of intelligence along with his measured optimism about what it can do. As Thomas sees it, the human animal is specified by a capacity for self-awareness that makes possible self-determinations. This should ideally issue in an ascent to God through love concretized in action. So what Thomas asserts, in fact, is a firm intellectual framework for a life of love. He once observed that men need to know what to believe, what to wish for, and what to do (*In duo Praecepta Caritatis*, Prologue). But this presupposes that they can attain something of the truth, some equation of their thought with reality in some matters. Not that this is easy; but neither is it impossible. More than once Aquinas warns of the traps set for those who rely too heavily upon authority or upon their imaginations or who identify their own images and concepts with things. At the same time he remains tranquilly confident that some sure knowledge is possible even in the philosophical quest. For as he remarked in commenting on a catalogue of skeptics in Aristotle's *Metaphysics*, "If philosophers, who are supposed to be special lovers and seekers after truth and to attain as much of it as men can, should decide that truth cannot be found, how rightly would they mourn this frustration of their search" (*In lib. Meta.*, b. IV, lect. 12).

Since schools exist specifically, though by no means exclusively, for intellectual growth, they have at least a notional esteem for the mind, and they are only effective when this esteem is real. An anti-intellectual philosophy of education would contain a self-contradiction. If Thomas' emphasis on rationality were generally understood by contemporary social scientists, it would probably be criticized for paying too little attention to irrational forces, on the one hand, and to the molding of personality by social pressures, on the other. More usually, though, the Thomistic synthesis of Christian and Hellenic ideals is not really recognized. In a distinguished essay on liberal education, for instance, Daniel Bell contrasts the Greek aspiration toward virtue and reason with the Christian historical vision of man struggling with "sinful impulses, hopefully transfigured by the healing power of love." [10] This contrast would be persuasive were it limited, let us say, to Aristotle face-to-face with Augustine. But it quite forgets Thomas' anthropology, which aims at unifying both insights in a single, though complex, conception of the human condition.

A second worthwhile, though no longer exceptional, theme is embodied in Aquinas' theory of disposition, or *habitus,* which makes of all education a genuine ontological growth as the personality is enlarged through acquisition of abiding qualities or dispositions. You are not a scientist, according to this account, if you parrot conclusions, but only if you can show how these unroll from premises. You are not an artist if you produce a fine effect by chance, but only if you have developed the power to control your materials consistently. You are not good if you are merely coerced by another or by your neurosis, but only if you have freely conformed your behavior to your belief.

Contemporary educators would also find familiar and agreeable two further features of Thomas' thought: his emphasis upon the importance for the life of the mind of the bodily dimension generally and sensory experience particularly, and his appreciation of the instrumental character that, in turn, intellectual activity has in relation to the whole of life. For despite his intellectualism, Thomas does see intelligence as instrumental to the values of love and community.

A fifth theme, however, is less intelligible now than it was in the thirteenth century, which had what John Updike nicely described as a "fusion of faith and action, politics and culture, symbol and reality." [11] We have already noted that many Christians no longer think of fusion as a good way of harmonizing religious and secular

values in their lives. They judge that this sort of coales-
cence really ends in a confusion in which the religious is
compromised and the secular diminished. Yet they continue to cherish the ideal of a life and thought in which
both these zones are properly acknowledged and harmonized. This ideal is opposed equally to the secularistic
denial of any realities other than this world and to Tertullian's famous disclaimer, "After Jesus Christ we have
no need of speculation, after the Gospel no need of research." [12] It is rather the ideal for which another sec-
ond-century Christian devised a graceful image. For in
the *Exhortation to the Greeks* (*Protrepticus* 9), Clement
of Alexandria pictured the great Hellenic poets and philosophers joining the congregation of believers as so many
musicians playing in the one orchestra under the direction of Christ, the Word.

It is, of course, easier to create this sort of synthesis
in one's own thought than it is to construct an educational program for developing a similar synthesis in others. Thomas cannot be credited with that latter achievement, but he did elaborate a world view in which the
Gospel and secular culture were harmonized. When he
wishes to talk about divine "grace," for instance, he em-
ploys the Aristotelian concept of a disposition. One
must admit that the Christian schoolmasters of the sixteenth century, whether Catholic or Protestant, did not
bring off any similar synthesis of faith and Renaissance
humanism, of piety and letters, as they would have said,
although they earnestly wished to do so.[13]

Twentieth-century Christians, in their turn, cannot
aim at restoring the Thomistic synthesis as though it
were some ideological Williamsburg. But they can take
heart from Thomas' example and try to find their own
way to a new relating of wisdom and belief. This must
necessarily take account of the deepened understanding
of man's social dimension that has been gained in the
last hundred or more years. Marx's *Sixth Thesis on*

Feuerbach declared that the human essence is the en-
semble of social relations. This is only partly true, for if
there are relationships, there must be centers that are related to one another. But it does serve to emphasize the
prime importance of that core of relationships that defines and constitutes so much of what we are. This theme
has been effectively set forth in the United States by
such thinkers as Cooley, Mead, and Dewey. They have
drawn attention to the unfolding of human personality
in terms of social living from the moment that family
life begins to stimulate and support the first flowering of
motor activity, speech, manners, and virtue.

This perception is found in Aquinas only in the most
rudimentary form. His metaphysical reflections on relationship consider this category so abstractly that he can
call it the weakest of all realities—*ens debilissimum* (*De
Pot.*, VII, 9). Often enough, it is true, he adverts to the
indispensability of society for the individual but only
very briefly. Besides, these passages leave the reader with
the impression that the individual is thought of as standing over against society, which he needs somewhat as he
would need transportation for travel. There is not here
the accent of another great Italian priest-philosopher who
would write seven hundred years after Thomas:

> Society is not an entity or an organism outside and above
> the individual, nor is the individual a reality outside and
> above society. Man is at once individual and social. His
> individual potentiality and his social potentiality have a
> single root in his sensitive-rational nature. He is so indi-
> vidual as not to partake of any life but his own, as to be
> an incommunicable personality. He is so social that he
> could not exist nor develop his faculties nor even live his
> life outside the social forms.[14]

In the history of Western political thought, however,
Thomas is a significant figure because he advanced the

Aristotelian thesis that man is naturally social, so that political society is a necessary expression of his nature rather than a condition induced by his fall from grace, as the Augustinian tradition held. "The political community (*civitas*)," Thomas wrote in the Prologue to the *Commentary on the Politics*, "is the chief among the constructions of human reason for all the other human communities are referred to it . . . So among the practical sciences, politics is the principal one which structures all the others since it deals with the last and highest of values in human affairs" (*In lib. Pol.*, Prooemium). It is, of course, final only within the horizon of this world, not unconditionally so. For in Thomas' view the ultimate goal of men is that union with God that transcends the temporal order.

This Thomistic political thought is itself a formidable topic to which books have been devoted. Here it is enough to note the Aristotelian dictum that provides its rationale: The philosophy of politics completes the philosophy of man. This is the sixth and last of the themes we wanted to note. It reminds us that no full theory of education is developed without a theory of society. But theories differ even as societies do—some being oppressive and others true communities of friendship. It all depends upon the values that the group cherishes and about which it is organized. So we may conclude with a last word from St. Thomas Aquinas himself:

Insofar as men judge differently about the goal of human life, so will they judge differently about the character of their social life together. Those who make pleasure or power or prestige their goal, will think that the best of societies in which they can live pleasurably or amass riches or honors or control over others. But those who put a premium upon virtue as the purpose of this earthly life will think that the best of societies in which men can best live together in peace and goodness [In lib. Pol., b. II, lect. 1].

<> NOTES <>

1. Ida Friederike Görres, *Broken Lights: Diaries and Letters 1951–1959,* trans. Barbara Waldstein-Wartenberg (Westminster, Md.: Newman Press, 1964), p. 87.

2. Raymond J. Nogar, O.P., *The Lord of the Absurd* (New York: Herder and Herder, 1966), p. 125.

3. Dorothy L. Sayers, *The Poetry of Search and the Poetry of Statement* (London: Gollancz, 1963), pp. 8–9.

4. See Mark De Wolfe Howe, ed., *Holmes-Laski Letters: The Correspondence of Mr. Justice Holmes and Harold J. Laski 1916–1935* (Cambridge: Harvard University Press, 1953), Vol. II, p. 900.

5. The translation is that of Thomas Gilby, *St. Thomas Aquinas: Philosophical Texts* (London: Oxford University Press, 1951), n. 656, p. 247.

6. This observation is made by the translator previously cited, Anthony Kenny, *St. Thomas Aquinas: Summa Theologiae: Volume 22: Dispositions for Human Acts* (New York: McGraw-Hill, 1964), Introduction, p. xix.

7. See Joseph de Finance, S.J., "Being and Subjectivity," trans. W. Norris Clarke, S.J., *Cross Currents,* 6 (1956), 163–178; and Robert O. Johann, S.J., "Subjectivity," *The Review of Metaphysics,* 12 (1958), 200–234.

8. J. V. Langmead Casserley, *Apologetics and Evangelism* (Philadelphia: Westminster Press, 1962), p. 155.

9. In his own life, of course, St. Thomas was a teacher endlessly generous with his time and energies for the service of his students, as Joseph Pieper points out in a few eloquent pages of his little book, *The Silence of St. Thomas,* trans. John Murray, S.J., and Daniel O'Connor (Chicago: Regnery, 1965), pp. 22–25.

10. Daniel Bell, *The Reforming of General Education* (New York: Columbia University Press, 1966), p. 150.

11. John Updike, "Books: Two Points on a Descending Curve," *The New Yorker* (January 7, 1967), p. 91.

12. Tertullian (ca. 160–230), *De Praescriptionibus Haereticorum*, vii. 9–13, trans. S. L. Greenslade, *Early Latin Theology*, Vol. V, *The Library of Christian Classics* (London: SCM Press, 1956), p. 36.

13. See on this point the essay by F. H. Hilliard, "The Legacy of Christianity in the Schools," in F. H. Hilliard, *et al.*, *Christianity in Education* (London: Allen & Unwin, 1966), pp. 27–28.

14. Luigi Sturzo, *Inner Laws of Society: A New Sociology*, trans. Barbara Barclay Carter (New York: P. J. Kenedy and Sons, 1944), p. xiv. Don Sturzo (1871–1959) was both scholar and man of affairs who in 1919 founded an Italian "Popular Party," which Mussolini subsequently banned. It was revived under De Gasperi after World War II as the Christian Democratic Party.

Bibliographical
Note

The general reader making his first approach to Thomism is usually looking for a book that is short, readily available, and in English. He will probably find the most useful introduction to Aquinas' life, times, and thought in Josef Pieper's *Guide to Thomas Aquinas,* trans. Richard and Clara Winston (New York: Pantheon Books, 1962). This is also available in softcover edition as a Mentor-Omega Book. Vernon J. Bourke's *Aquinas' Search for Wisdom* (Milwaukee: Bruce, 1965) is a sober summary of the known facts about St. Thomas and his period and includes some introduction to his ideas. M. -D. Chenu, O.P., in *Toward Understanding Saint Thomas,* trans. A. -M. Landry, O.P., and D. Hughes, O.P. (Chicago: Regnery, 1964) summarizes the biographical data much more briefly but gives a full and valuable account of Thomas' technical language, literary forms, methods, and various writings. If one wants a short study of the life itself there is a book by the ranking contemporary biographer, Angelus Walz, O.P., *Saint Thomas Aquinas: A Biographical Study,* trans. Sebastian Bullough, O.P. (Westminster, Md.: Newman, 1951). Three brief studies concentrating on the philosophical side of Thomas' thought are: F. C. Copleston, *Aquinas* (Baltimore: Penguin, 1955); Paul Grenet, *Tho-*

mism: An Introduction, trans. James F. Ross (New York: Harper & Row, 1967); and an older work first published in 1931 and reissued in 1956, A. D. Sertillanges, O.P., *Foundations of Thomistic Philosophy,* trans. Godfrey Anstruther, O.P. (Springfield, Ill.: Templegate, 1956). Two instructive, chapter-length statements can be found in David Knowles, *The Evolution of Medieval Thought* (Baltimore: Helicon, 1962), pp. 255–268, and Etienne Gilson, *History of Christian Philosophy in the Middle Ages* (New York: Random House, 1955), pp. 361–383. Gilson is also the author of the outstanding longer study, *The Christian Philosophy of St. Thomas Aquinas,* trans. L. K. Shook, C.S.B. (New York: Random House, 1956). This volume also contains a descriptive catalogue of Thomas' works and other bibliographical information. For a general bibliographical guide to the study of Thomism covering the period 1920–1940, see Vernon J. Bourke, *Thomistic Bibliography: 1920–1940* (St. Louis: Modern Schoolman, 1945).

The nonspecialist who wants to sample directly the range and flavor of Thomas' writings can do so in two volumes of brief texts which have been selected, arranged under topical headings and attractively translated by Thomas Gilby: *St. Thomas Aquinas: Philosophical Texts* (London: Oxford, 1951) and *St. Thomas Aquinas: Theological Texts* (London: Oxford, 1955). A two-volume collection of longer passages is that edited by Anton C. Pegis, *Basic Writings of St. Thomas* (New York: Random House, 1945). Father Gilby is the general editor of a new translation of the *Summa Theologiae,* whose volumes, with the Latin text and the English translation on facing pages, are being brought out in the United States by McGraw-Hill. An older translation by the English Dominican Fathers, originally published in London in twenty-two volumes, was reissued in a large, three-volume American edition (New York: Benziger, 1947 and 1948). The *Summa contra Gentiles* was translated, under the title *On the Truth of the Catholic Faith,* by James F. Anderson, Vernon J. Bourke, Charles J. O'Neill, and Anton C. Pegis (Garden City, N.Y.: Hanover House, 1955, 1957) in 5 volumes.

For a full bibliography of books and articles on Thomistic educational theory, see Tad W. Guzie, S.J., *The Analogy of Learning: An Essay Toward a Thomistic Psychology of Learning* (New York: Sheed and Ward, 1960), pp. 1–25, 225–236. Aquinas' *Quaestiones Disputatae de Veritate* have been translated by Robert W. Mulligan, S.J., James V. McGlynn, S.J., and Robert W. Schmidt, S.J., and published in three volumes under the title *Truth* (Chicago: Regnery, 1952, 1954). From this translation the eleventh of the questions, the *De Magistro,* has been issued separately as *Thomas Aquinas: The Teacher* (Chicago: Regnery, 1954). There is an older translation, with extensive commentary, of the *De Magistro* by Mary Helen Mayer, *The Philosophy of Teaching of St. Thomas Aquinas* (Milwaukee: Bruce, 1929). A good essay on the *De Magistro* is by G. J. Shannon, C.M., "Aquinas on the Teacher's Art," *The Clergy Review,* XXXI (June, 1949), 375–385; and it is also given some perceptive pages in A. C. F. Beales, *Education Under Penalty: English Catholic Education from the Reformation to the Fall of James II* (London: The Athlone Press, University of London, 1963), pp. 5–7. A more general essay is by W. Lawson, S.J., "Neo-Thomism," in A. V. Judges, ed., *Education and the Philosophic Mind* (London: Harrap, 1957), pp. 43–59. The most distinguished writings on education by a Thomist, however, are those of Jacques Maritain. Extracts from them and bibliographical information will be found in Donald and Idella Gallagher, eds., *The Education of Man: The Educational Philosophy of Jacques Maritain* (Garden City, N.Y.: Doubleday, 1962).

Index